Pl

A golden collection of tender words and charming wit from the heart of the family. Simple truths of home life, growing up and days-gone-by have been compiled to bring joy and inspiration to each day.

Some material for this book has been collected from many sources and original authors are unknown. Regretfully, credit cannot be attributed to those authors.

Going Home™
© Copyright 1994 LIGHTEN UP ENTERPRISES, INC.
5223 Edina Industrial Blvd.
Edina, MN 55439-2910
ISBN 1-879127-34-2

Look for these titles by Lighten Up Enterprises, Inc. at your favorite gift shop, sacred or secular bookstore.

Heart Delights®
Heart to Heart
Friend to Friend®
Teacher's Delights™
Celebrate Today®
Treat Yourself®
Crafts All Together™
Together in the Kitchen™
Minnesota in My Heart™
Hugs For The Heart®
Heart Delights for Mothers & Daughters®
Heart Delights for Fathers & Sons®
Running Starts for Teen Hearts®

Lighten Up…Inspirations for Dieters™
Heart Delights for the Golden Years®
Together as a Family™
Celebrate Treasures of Friendship™
Georgia In My Heart™
Texas in my Heart®
The Best of Hearts™
Places of the Heart Series:
Going Home™
Main Street Memories™
Lessons from the Heart™
Simple Treasures™

JANUARY 1

True housekeeping implies homekeeping. Housekeeping is a science to be studied, an art to be practiced and a grace to be developed. It comprehends all that goes into making a home.

— The Housekeeper Cookbook, 1884

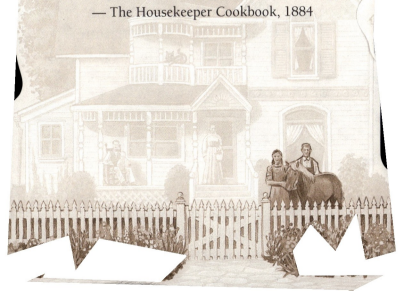

DECEMBER 31

If there is righteousness in the heart
there will be beauty in the character.
If there be beauty in the character,
there will be harmony in the home.
If there is harmony in the home,
there will be order in the nation.
When there is order in the nation,
there will be peace in the world.

— Chinese proverb

JANUARY 2

The law of heredity is that all undesirable traits come from the other parent.

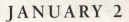

Setting a good example for your children takes all the fun out of middle age.

DECEMBER 30

Let us not look back in anger,
nor forward in fear,
but around in awareness.
— James Thurber

*One thing about mischievous kids
is that they get their parents
home from the party.*

JANUARY 3

There was this man who wasn't exactly athletic — he got winded turning on the TV set.

Adults are obsolete children.
— *Dr. Seuss*

DECEMBER 29

A New Year's resolution is one
that goes in one year
and out the other.

*What makes you tolerant of a neighbor's party
is being invited there.*

JANUARY 4

Why can't our neighbors do as we do,
and shut their eyes to our faults?

*If you can't get rid of the family skeleton,
you might as well make it dance.*

DECEMBER 28

A small house will hold
as much happiness as a big one.

The sweetest revenge is to forgive.

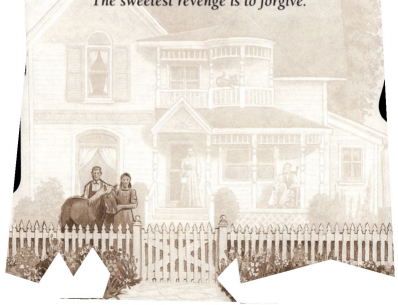

JANUARY 5

These days, it can be said there's too much water in our chlorine supply.

Home is where you don't have to make reservations in advance.

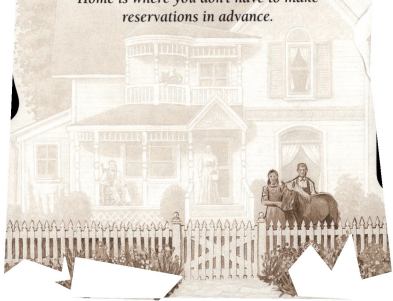

DECEMBER 27

Keep your ideals
high enough to inspire you
and low enough to encourage you.

*One popular way to plan an estate
is to spend it in retirement.*

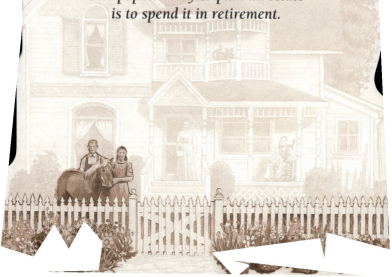

JANUARY 6

There is a sure way to keep visitors away from your house — sell the house.

In the moving business "fragile" really means "slam dunk."

DECEMBER 26

The people who are hardest
to convince they're at the retirement age
are children at bedtime.

*The ornaments of a home
are the family members who frequent it.*

JANUARY 7

Nostalgia is longing for a place you said you'd never move back to.

Flattery won't hurt you if you don't swallow it.

DECEMBER 25

Here's to the blessings
of the year,
Here's to friends and family
we hold so dear,
To peace on earth both far
and near.

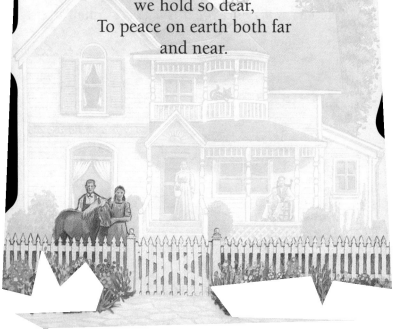

JANUARY 8

There are times when being a parent feels like you are feeding the hand that bites you.

What you don't owe won't hurt you.

DECEMBER 24

Don't worry about the size of your Christmas tree. In the eyes of a child, they're all 25 feet tall.

The best Christmas gift of all is the presence of a happy family all wrapped up with one another.

JANUARY 9

Tell a child he is brave
and you help that child become so.

*Middle age is when weightlifting
consists of standing up.*

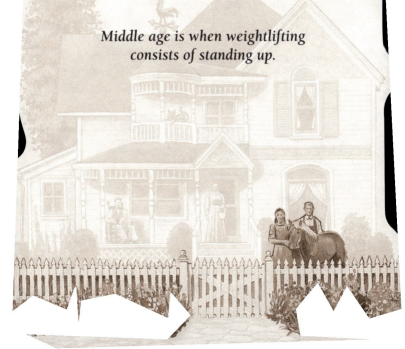

DECEMBER 23

I don't believe I ever heard anyone say
they wanted a Christmas card
for Christmas.

*The exchange of gifts should be reciprocal
rather than retaliatory.*

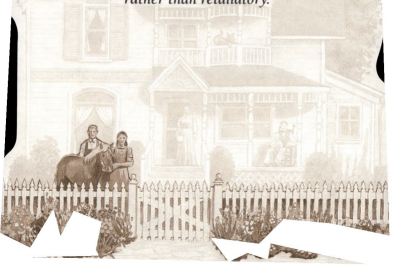

JANUARY 10

Adam may have had his troubles, but he never had to listen to Eve talk about the other men she could have married.

If you think old soldiers fade away, try getting in an old army uniform!

DECEMBER 22

What most people want for Christmas is two more weeks to prepare for it.

Home is where the college student home for the holidays isn't.

JANUARY 11

It's hard to comprehend the sense of values of some folks. They'll leave a $20,000 car sitting out in a snow storm but the children's $20 sled must be parked in the garage.

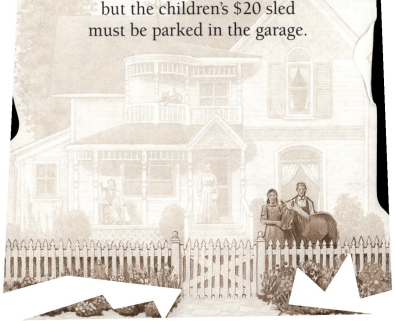

DECEMBER 21

The difference between adults and children is adults have toys that require monthly payments.

The first thing a child learns when he gets a drum is that he's never going to get another one.

JANUARY 12

Romance is cooking up a gourmet meal;
reality is washing the dishes afterwards.

*The way things go wrong with the family car,
the ideal second car should be a tow truck.*

DECEMBER 20

The best gift for the family
that has everything
is a burglar alarm!

Give a pet — no assembly required.

JANUARY 13

The older we get, the better we were.

Times are so bad, parents are writing to their kids in college to send money home.

DECEMBER 19

The only thing some family members
have in common is a key
to their front door.

*The trouble with being punctual
is that nobody's there to appreciate it.*

JANUARY 14

A Chinese philosopher once said that parents who are afraid to "put their foot down" usually have children who step on toes.

A budget is just another name for a family quarrel.

DECEMBER 18

Everything in a household runs smoothly
when love oils the machinery.

*Persons are to be loved;
things are to be used.*

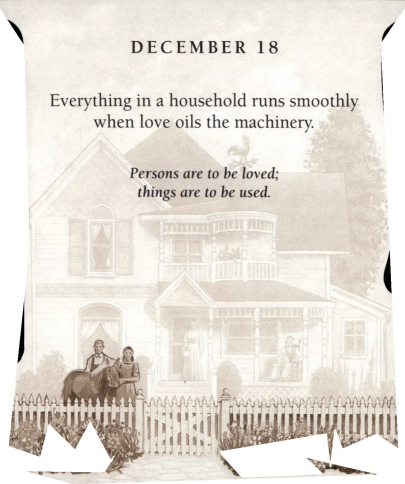

JANUARY 15

RECIPE FROM DAYS GONE BY:
PRAIRIE COFFEE

1 pint corn meal
½ c. molasses
1 pint wheat flour
1 teaspoon salt,
Water for stiff dough

Mix, roll thin, cut out like yeast cakes; put in a pan to dry in the oven. When thoroughly dry, brown very dark. To use, put 2 or 3 of the cakes and 1 tablespoon of the coffee in the pot, pour on boiling water, let boil and settle.

DECEMBER 17

Forgiveness warms the heart
and cools the sting.

A loving family will joyfully sing when you are on top of a mountain, and silently walk beside you through the valley.

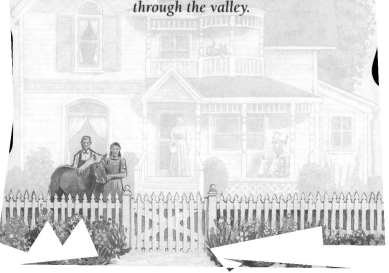

JANUARY 16

Television: A medium, so called,
because it is neither rare nor well-done.
— Ernie Kovaks

*The best place to send kids during the summer:
Camp Grandparents.*

DECEMBER 16

Parents were invented to make children happy by giving them something to ignore.

*If you can laugh at it —
you can live with it.*

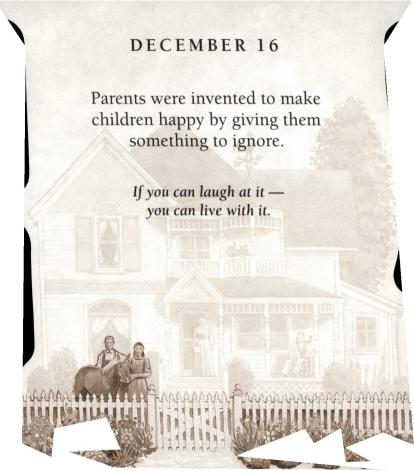

JANUARY 17

When someone says,
"I don't want to mention any names,"
it isn't necessary.

*Children cannot understand adult logic.
Why does a kid have to go to sleep
when mom's tired?*

DECEMBER 15

The idea of fingerprinting children
is a good one. It will settle the question
as to who used the guest towel
in the bathroom.

*Patience is a quality most needed
when it is exhausted.*

JANUARY 18

Why is it the first gray hairs stick out straight?

Going home is facing the past with knowledge of the future.

DECEMBER 14

May you never forget
what is worth remembering,
or remember what is best forgotten.

*The best time to save money for retirement
is when you have some.*

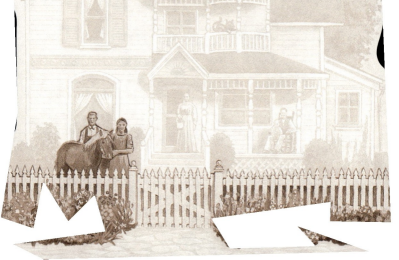

JANUARY 19

If you have had enough of your friend,
lend him some money.
— Russian proverb

*What people really wanted from Moses
was an 11th commandment that said,
"Disregard the other commandments."*

DECEMBER 13

Favorite Author
"Who's your favorite author, Tommy?"
"My dad."
"What does he write?"
"Checks!"

JANUARY 20

If you sleep in a chair
You have nothing to lose,
But a nap at the wheel
Is a permanent snooze.

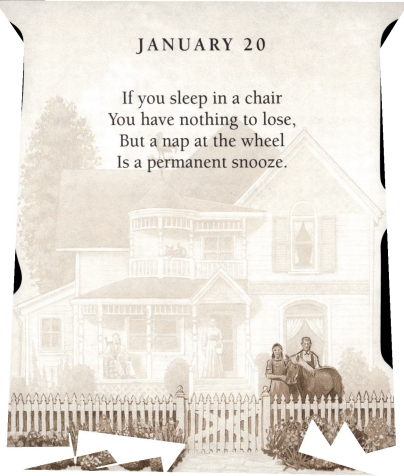

DECEMBER 12

Today, teenagers are people
who express a strong desire to be different
by dressing exactly alike.

If it hurts, don't wear it.

JANUARY 21

Marriages are made in heaven,
and very few ever get back to the factory.

*For some, cooking is a religious experience.
Everything they make is a sacrifice
or a burnt offering.*

DECEMBER 11

It's easy to spot new parents.
They're the ones who carry baby pictures
in their wallet instead of money.

*Children's tears — the most effective
water power in the world.*

JANUARY 22

There seems to be an excess of everything except parking spaces and religion.

Be sure you're home when opportunity knocks, or it may take your TV set.

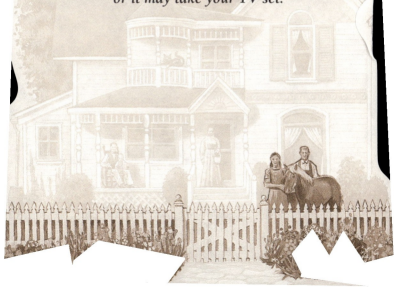

DECEMBER 10

One good turn, and you have most of the bed covers.

It's hard to raise a family — especially in the morning.

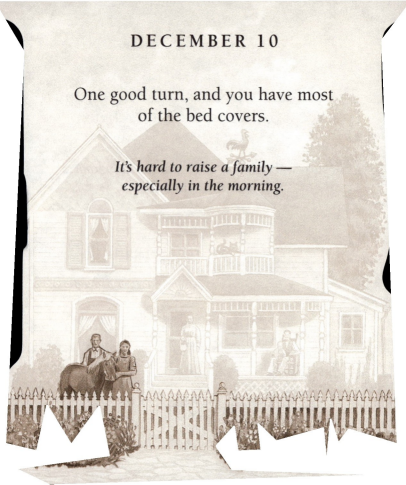

JANUARY 23

What's worse than finding one good glove from that pair you lost?

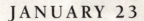

Never hire an electrician with a singed eyebrow to do home repair.

DECEMBER 9

If parents want to see what children can do,
they must stop giving them things.

*We make a living by what we get,
but we make a life by what we give.*

JANUARY 24

Respect a child, and that child will respect you.

A successful person is one who solves more problems than he creates.

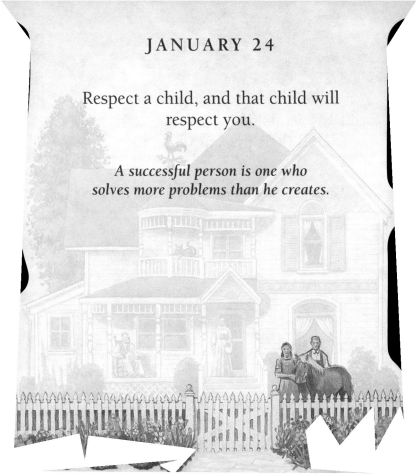

DECEMBER 8

The holidays are when everyone
wants their past forgotten
and their present remembered.

Words you have to eat can be hard to digest.

JANUARY 25

Remember the old days when you threatened to move if the landlord didn't do something to improve the place?

It's difficult for a five-foot-nine father to impress upon his six-foot-one son why junk food is bad for the body.

DECEMBER 7

Learn from the mistakes of others.
You can't live long enough
to make them all yourself.

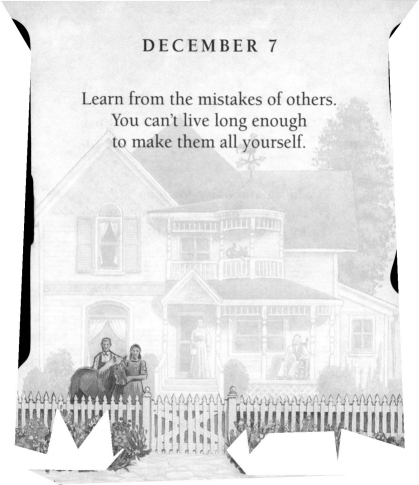

JANUARY 26

A good day is when the wheels of your shopping cart all go in the same direction.

Remember the days when radios plugged in and toothbrushes didn't?

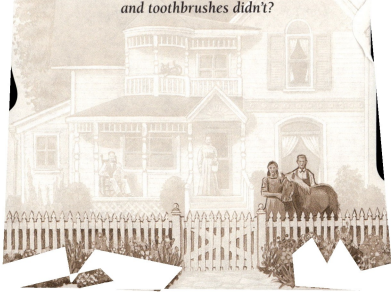

DECEMBER 6

Middle age: When you can do
just as much as ever,
but would rather not.

*Don't we all admire the wisdom of people
who ask us for advice?*

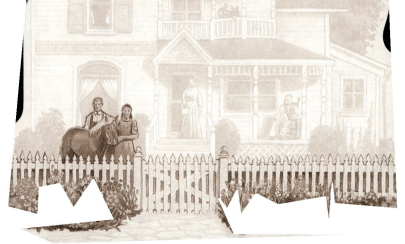

JANUARY 27

The funniest joke in the world is often the truth.

Today, there are four basic food groups: fresh, frozen, fast and junk!

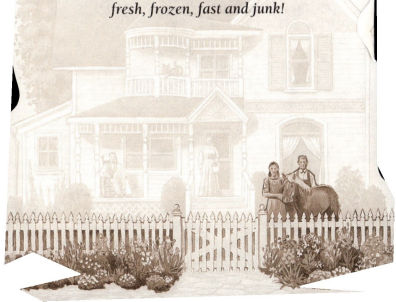

DECEMBER 5

No matter how many lives we're given,
most of us would ask for one more.

*Cherish all your happy times together;
they make a soft pillow for old age.*

JANUARY 28

A family is composed of children,
parents, an occasional animal,
and the common cold.
— Ogden Nash

*Heirlooms are all the things
a grandmother wanted more than money.*

DECEMBER 4

The big food companies are working on a tearless onion and they probably will do it. They've already given us tasteless bread.

Many parents would learn to cook if they weren't so busy trying to prepare meals.

JANUARY 29

If your spouse laughs at your jokes,
you either have some good jokes
or you have a loving spouse.

*Middle age is when work is a lot more fun
and fun is a lot more work.*

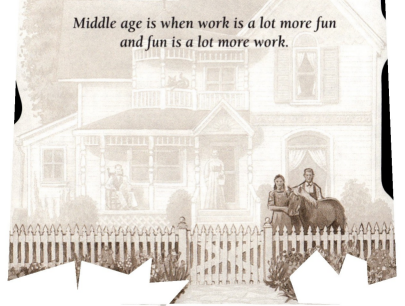

DECEMBER 3

A lasting gift to a child
is the gift of a parent's listening ear —
and heart.

*The hand that rocks the cradle
charges $5.00 an hour.*

JANUARY 30

After you lose your membership in it,
the younger generation seems pretty bad.

*Some families can't save up for a rainy day.
One good drizzle would wipe them out.*

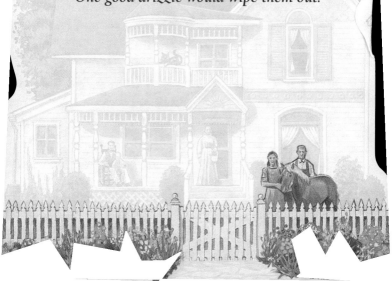

DECEMBER 2

If you believe the world's population is getting older, you haven't spent much time at a shopping mall on a weekend.

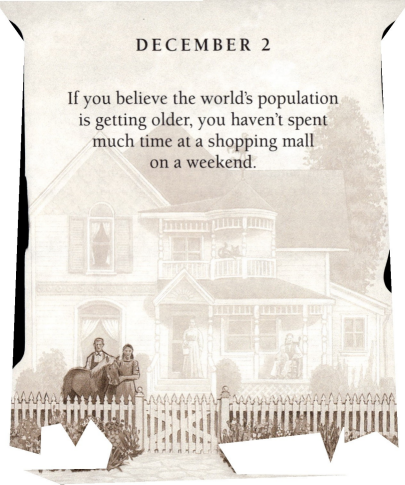

JANUARY 31

What's confusing about our life story
is that the plot began
before we came on the scene.

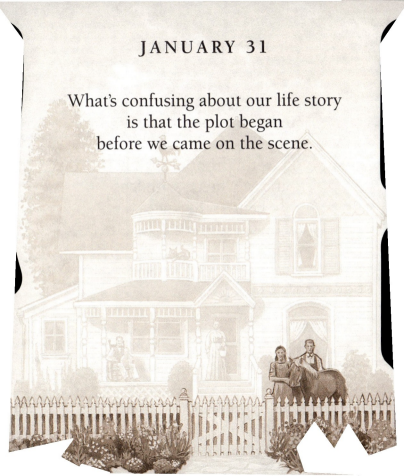

DECEMBER 1

Do not lean on the table,
and avoid noisy behavior.
Keep elbows close to the side
and feet in front of the chair.
Sit easily erect, with legs
bent at the knee.

— The Housekeeper Cookbook, 1884

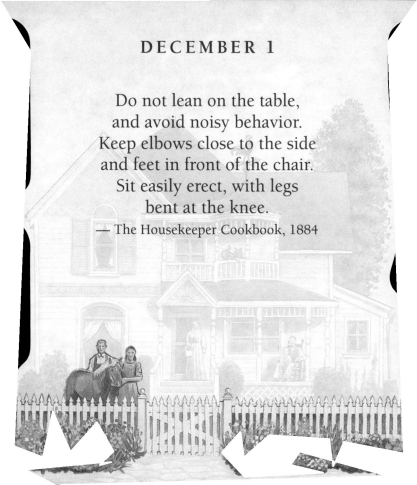

FEBRUARY 1

Right knowledge, with good common sense,
must unite with love in planning
for the entire well-being of the family,
or life will become like sweet bells jangled,
out of tune.

— The Housekeeper Cookbook, 1884

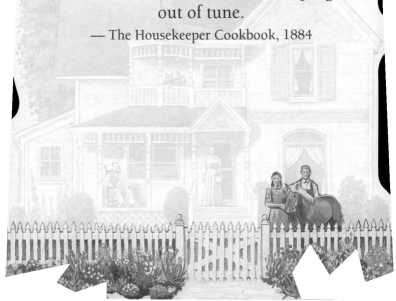

NOVEMBER 30

On days when it is cold and wet
Our children watch the TV set
In just the way the darlings do
When it is warm and skies are blue.

FEBRUARY 2

Monotony is the awful reward
of the careful.

*Mother is the name of God
in the eyes of children.*

NOVEMBER 29

The beauty of the house is order;
The blessing of the house is contentment;
The glory of the house is hospitality;
The crown of the house is godliness.

— Fireplace motto

FEBRUARY 3

If evolution is really true,
how come mothers only have two hands?

*Many a family that seems to be on Easy Street
in only on Easy Payment Street.*

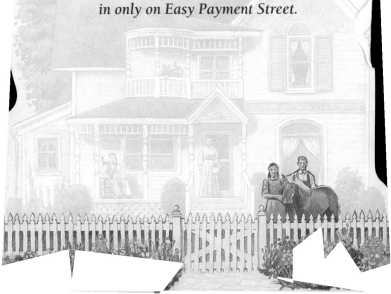

NOVEMBER 28

Our undeserved failures may surprise us,
but our undeserved successes
surprise us more.

*A smile on your face is the light in the window
that tells people you are home.*

FEBRUARY 4

Words, once spoken, can never be recalled.

The fine art of being a parent consists of sleeping when the baby isn't looking.

NOVEMBER 27

Home is the place we have to leave
to appreciate good food and good beds.

*Going home is difficult
if your parents own a motor home.*

FEBRUARY 5

A good way to save face is to keep the lower half shut.

Every now and then we see a television program that makes us yearn for the good old days of static radio.

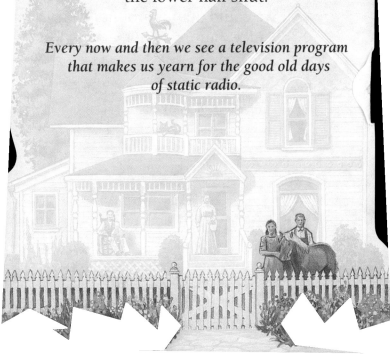

NOVEMBER 26

A stroll down memory lane
would be wonderful
if we could detour around
a few bumpy roads.

*Everyone should keep a grave to bury
the faults of their family.*

FEBRUARY 6

Key to longevity:
Keep breathing.
— Sophie Tucker

Your dream house is much easier to maintain as a dream.

NOVEMBER 25

A real home is more
than just a roof over your head —
it is a foundation under your feet.

FEBRUARY 7

Love your neighbor,
yet don't pull down your hedge.
— Ben Franklin

Have you heard about the new teenaged doll?
You wind it up and it resents you for it.

NOVEMBER 24

It is indeed a desirable thing
to be well descended,
but the glory belongs to our ancestors.
— Plutarch

Our favorite attitude should be gratitude.

FEBRUARY 8

The problem with some teenagers
is not having another mouth to feed,
it's having another mouth to listen to.

*An egoist is someone who is always
me-deep in conversation.*

NOVEMBER 23

We won't continue having a horn of plenty if we keep blowing it.

The family that eats together gets fat.

FEBRUARY 9

How come the husbands of the ten best-dressed women are never on the list of the ten best-dressed men?

There's a great new device for TV weathermen. It's called a window.

NOVEMBER 22

Some families can trace their ancestry
back three hundred years,
but can't tell you where
their children were last night.

*The best thing to give someone
is a chance.*

FEBRUARY 10

Nothing lasts forever except a bad movie.

The trouble with getting rid of the TV
is that no one can remember
what they used to do before it came along.

NOVEMBER 21

It isn't what you have in your pocket
that makes you thankful,
but what you have in your heart.

FEBRUARY 11

Parents don't bring up children anymore.
They finance them.

What's the longest period of time?
One payday to the next!

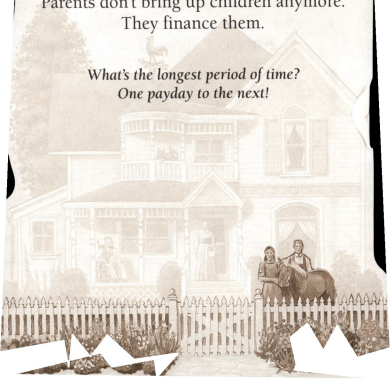

NOVEMBER 20

Remember when family meals were carefully thought out instead of thawed out?

Good character is like a good meal — it's usually homemade.

FEBRUARY 12

If you're trying to remember when your
child called from college,
just look in your checkbook.

*You can always tell the family
that has everything.
It's in the station wagon when they
start their vacation.*

NOVEMBER 19

Cleaning your house while kids are still growing is like shoveling the walk before it stops snowing.

*To be happy at home
is the ultimate aim of all ambition.*

FEBRUARY 13

The best birthdays of all
are those that haven't arrived yet.

*Every family member should share the chores.
One child washes the dishes
and the other sweeps them up.*

NOVEMBER 18

You know your children are growing up when they start asking questions that have answers.

FEBRUARY 14

Being in love is like a state
of perpetual anesthesia.

Let the early bird catch the worm.
Wait a bit and order French toast.

NOVEMBER 17

Another thing to be thankful for
is that most people do their worst driving
on the golf course.

*What most families need are fewer rules
and more good examples.*

FEBRUARY 15

RECIPES FROM DAYS GONE BY:
POTATO NUTS

Pare raw potatoes, cut them in balls, with a vegetable cutter and throw them into cold water. Drain, throw them in salted boiling water for 5 minutes, skim them out, drain dry and put into a hot spider with plenty of butter. Shake them around, and set the spider into the oven to brown the potatoes. Salt and serve. Or, cook in boiling lard, drain, salt, and serve.

NOVEMBER 16

An antique is a piece of furniture which you have finally made the last payment on.

Many people mistake a short memory for a clear conscience.

FEBRUARY 16

The best time for parents to put their children to bed is when they still have the strength.

*Some parents age 25 years
while their children only age from 13 to 19.*

NOVEMBER 15

RECIPE FROM DAYS GONE BY:
BERLIN WREATHS

1 lb. washed butter	½ lb. white sugar
2 lbs. flour	4 eggs, yolks
4 hard boiled eggs, yolks	

Mix flour and sugar well together, then work in the butter and yolks of eggs. Cut the mixture into 6-inch strips, which should be round and as thick as a finger. Lap the ends, dip the cakes into beaten whites, then into coarse sugar, place on buttered tins and bake a light brown. They will keep a year and be just as good at last as at first.

FEBRUARY 17

Some people are so boring,
they make you feel like you wasted
an entire day in five minutes.

*A golfer yells fore,
takes 6, and puts down 5.*

NOVEMBER 14

A good way to find out
what the neighbors are doing
is to entertain their children.

*The only people who really listen
when the family argues
are the neighbors.*

FEBRUARY 18

The people who seem young
are those who never reveal their rage.

Living your life by the inch is a cinch,
but by the yard it's hard.

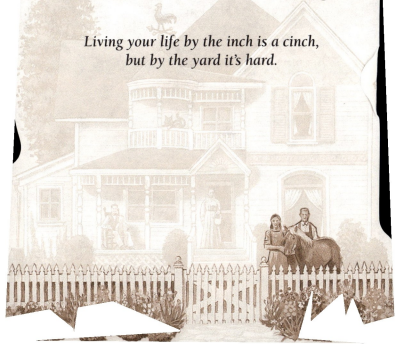

NOVEMBER 13

We can't say the car is old,
but it's the first time we've ever seen
bifocal headlights.

*Our memory is the treasure and guardian
of all things.*

FEBRUARY 19

One of the advantages of marriage is that you can't do something stupid without hearing about it.

It's a special person who can receive without forgetting and give without remembering.

NOVEMBER 12

Saying "Gesundheit!" doesn't really help
the common cold —
but it's about as good as anything
the doctors have come up with.

*A loving family and good health
are a man's best wealth.*

FEBRUARY 20

Half of our troubles can be traced
to saying "yes" too often
and not saying "no" soon enough.

*Bad habits may seem like small twigs
but may actually be big unbending branches.*

NOVEMBER 11

There's nothing much wrong
with the younger generation
that being a parent won't cure.

*Some babies start eating solids very early —
keys, bits of newspaper, pencils.*

FEBRUARY 21

High heels were invented by a man who always got kissed on the chin.

Everyone needs to be loved, especially when they don't deserve it.

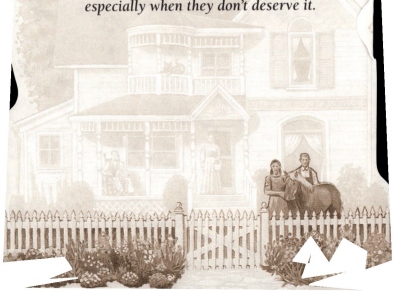

NOVEMBER 10

Talking to yourself is all right,
as long as you listen.

*As people grow older,
they talk less and say more.*

FEBRUARY 22

It's ironic that by the time our children
realize their parents were right
about a lot of things, they have children of
their own who think they're all wrong.

*A lot of us have seen the light,
but for many of us it's the one
inside the refrigerator.*

NOVEMBER 9

For some women, happiness is when the television tube blows out right at the start of the "Miss America Pageant."

TV has turned the family circle into a half circle.

FEBRUARY 23

Nothing draws a family closer together than a 12-inch TV set in a 9-ft. living room.

A cooperative worker does with a smile what he has to do anyway.

NOVEMBER 8

Always do right;
it will gratify some people
and astonish others.

*Only God is in a position
to look down on anyone.*

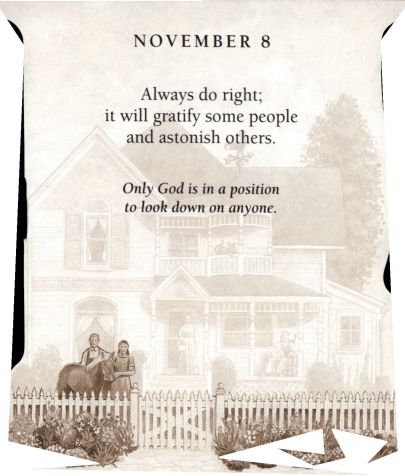

FEBRUARY 24

The principle objection to old age
is there's no future in it.

*A reputation is based not so much
on what you stand for,
as on what you fall for.*

NOVEMBER 7

We can be kept quite busy
trying to conceal the fact
that we don't know what we're doing.

FEBRUARY 25

Perched on the loftiest throne in the world,
we are still sitting on our own behind.

*It's confusing to everyone
if the rules of the house are multiple choice.*

NOVEMBER 6

America is a land where a citizen
will cross the ocean to fight for democracy,
but won't cross the street
to vote in an election.

*You have to say this about being poor —
it's inexpensive.*

FEBRUARY 26

Some folks let their yearnings exceed their earnings.

What you don't know won't help you much either.

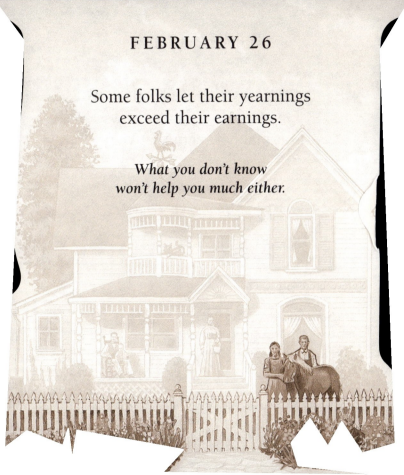

NOVEMBER 5

Is life really more complicated?
Or is it just the talk shows
that make it seem that way?

*Intelligence is hereditary,
you get it from your teenagers.*

FEBRUARY 27

Life is the greatest bargain;
we get it for nothing.
— Yiddish proverb

*Confidence is the feeling you have
before you fully understand the facts.*

NOVEMBER 4

A loving family strengthens with prayer, blesses with love and encourages with hope.

The warmth of a home is not necessarily determined by its heating system.

FEBRUARY 28

The best way to advise your kids
is to find out what they are going to do
and then advise them not to do it.

NOVEMBER 3

The younger we are, the more we want to change the world. The older we are the more we want to change the young.

Laughter is the shock absorber that eases the bumps of life.

FEBRUARY 29

If all fools wore white caps,
we would look like a flock of geese.

*The best throw of the dice
is to throw them away.*

NOVEMBER 2

The term "melting pot" used to mean the United States of America.
Now it means you put the wrong container in the microwave.

MARCH 1

The sweeping and dusting of a room seems simple enough, but is best done systematically. Begin from one corner and sweep toward the center with a short light stroke. The second time over, increase the length and force of the stroke, and the third, brush with long vigorous strokes.

— The Housekeeper Cookbook, 1884

NOVEMBER 1

Proper manners:
A gentleman takes his hat off to a lady,
and when with a lady raises it
when she recognizes a friend.
—The Housekeeper Cookbook, 1884

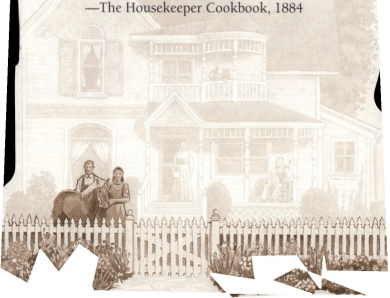

MARCH 2

The first 40 years of life give us the text;
the next 40 supply the commentary.

Most homes have closets for hanging clothes.
Kids use them when all the doorknobs are full.

OCTOBER 31

Some days the only thing
that goes off as planned
is the alarm clock.

Isn't it a greater life if you weaken a little?

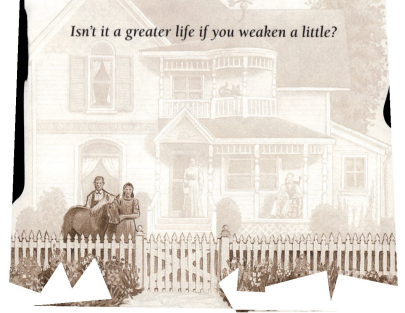

MARCH 3

The average mortgage runs about
30 years, which gives the owners time,
if they work on it every weekend,
to get the house in shape to sell.

*A smile is a curve that has
set many things straight.*

OCTOBER 30

Children may be
the investment of the future,
but grandchildren are the dividends.

*Where there is room in the heart,
there is always room in the house.*

MARCH 4

If you see a sign on a new high-rise apartment building announcing "Gracious Living" it can only mean one thing: "No Children Allowed."

OCTOBER 29

Psychiatric institutions are full of women whose homes were so spotless you could eat off the floor.

Domestic peace is that period of time between a child's bedtime and your own.

MARCH 5

If we didn't have ordinary people,
how could we tell the great ones?

*Though their pockets may be empty,
a couple is rich when they
fill each others' arms.*

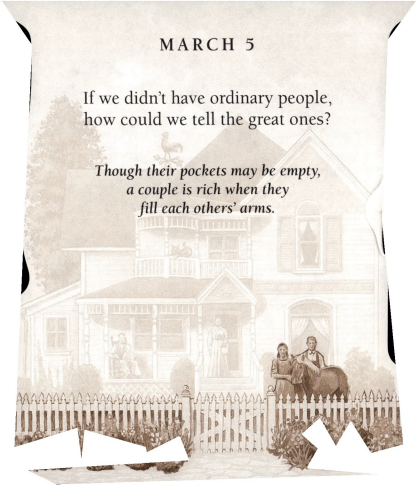

OCTOBER 28

Children are more apt to follow your lead
than the way you point.

*In every real man
is a child who wants to play.*

MARCH 6

The best years of a family are when the kids are too old to need a babysitter and too young to borrow the car.

Pedestrians are people without access to the family car.

OCTOBER 27

The family you come from isn't as important as the family you're going to have.

Happiness does not come from what you have, but from where you are.

MARCH 7

The difference between gossip and news depends on whether you hear it or tell it.

Problems are simply an opportunity to do your best.

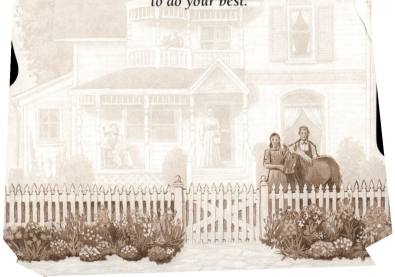

OCTOBER 26

When someone tells you,
"I run things at my house,"
it usually means the washing machine,
the vacuum cleaner and the dishwasher.

MARCH 8

A hospital should also have a recovery room adjoining the cashier's office.

There's no such thing as a sudden heart attack. It requires years of preparation.

OCTOBER 25

Our days are happier when we give people
a bit of our heart
rather than a piece of our mind.

*We like a friend who comes right out
and says what she thinks,
when she agrees with us.*

MARCH 9

Of two evils, when we tell ourselves
we are choosing the lesser,
we usually mean we are choosing
the more comfortable.

*In your hometown, friends and family
are the same people.*

OCTOBER 24

The kind of ancestors we have
is not as important as the kind
of descendants our children have.

*A mother is like a quilt
wrapped around the heart of a child.*

MARCH 10

A husband should try praising his wife even if it does startle her at first.

The best words parents can say to their kids: "We love you."

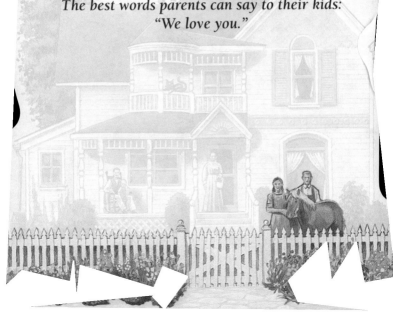

OCTOBER 23

Children need strength to lean on,
a shoulder to cry on,
and an example to learn from.

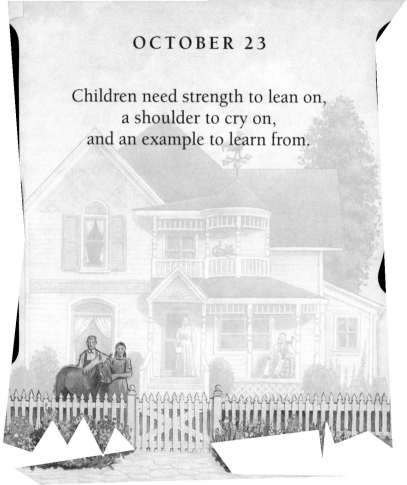

MARCH 11

Molecules are made of atoms.
Atoms are made of energy.
Energy is made from breakfast cereal.

Try sleeping when your teenager is out late.
You'll find you have a vivid imagination.

OCTOBER 22

For some the secret of dealing successfully
with a child is not to be his parent.

*The most profitable words
are those spent praising our children.*

MARCH 12

This is a very special day — it's the only one we will have all the way until tomorrow.

Influence is what many people think they have until they try to use it.

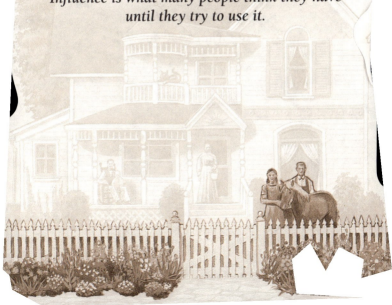

OCTOBER 21

Owning a home is the American dream.
Maintaining a home
provokes the American scream.

*People become well-to-do
by doing what they do well.*

MARCH 13

It's March.
Do you know where your receipts are?

*Let us all be happy and live within our means,
even if we have to borrow the money to do it.*
— Artemus Ward

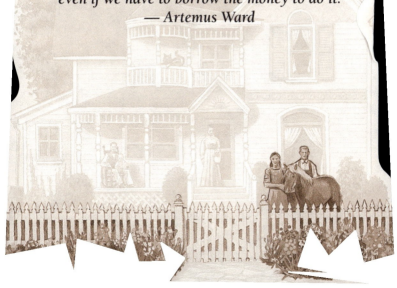

OCTOBER 20

What a father says to his children
is not heard by the world,
but it will be heard by posterity.

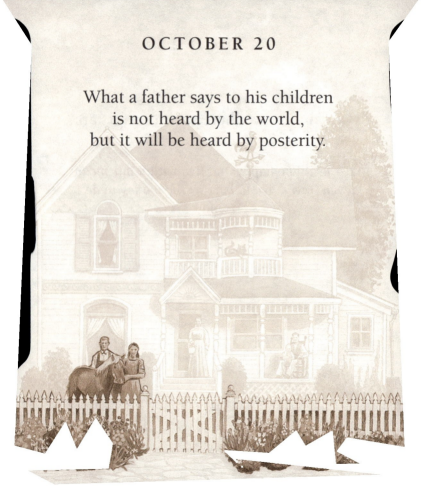

MARCH 14

Middle age is when you're faced with all kinds of temptations and you pick the one that gets you home by nine.

OCTOBER 19

The only good in pretending
is the fun we get out of fooling ourselves
that we fool somebody.

*Some family members don't mind suffering
as long as the rest of the family knows about it.*

MARCH 15

RECIPE FROM DAYS GONE BY:
ECONOMICAL SOUP

Roast beef bones
Turkey bones and dressing
Beefsteak bits
2 quarts water

Use any or all of the articles and cook slowly 2 hours. Take out the bones and strings, or strain the soup. If the turkey bones are used, a little chopped celery may be added with the beef bones and vegetables to suit the taste. The soup may be strained in that case and thickened with a little flour and water to which has been added salt and pepper. Serve with dry toast cut into fancy shapes.

OCTOBER 18

A great person is one
who can laugh at herself with others
and enjoy it as much as they do.

*Try to make all your mistakes early in the day —
while your mind is still fresh.*

MARCH 16

Housekeeping is like threading beads on a string with no knot at the end.

For many people, money talks.
— It says "See you later!"

OCTOBER 17

At the age of twenty we don't care
what the world thinks of us;
at thirty we worry about
what it thinks of us;
at forty we discover
that it isn't thinking of us at all.

MARCH 17

Those who are willing
need not wait to be called.

*If you don't have enough to do,
it can seem like a long time
from birth to death.*

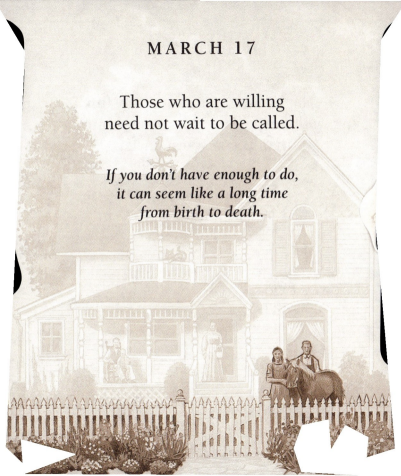

OCTOBER 16

Happy laughter and family fun will keep more children at home than the strictest curfew.

*A great man is he
who does not lose his child's heart.*
— *Mencius*

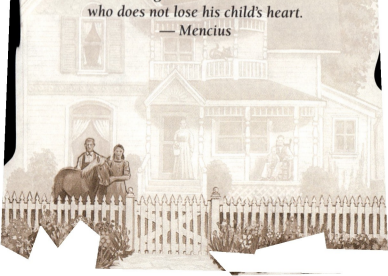

MARCH 18

There are those who sow their wild oats on Saturday night — then on Sunday pray for crop failure.

Praise youth and it will prosper.
— Irish Proverb

OCTOBER 15

RECIPE FROM DAYS GONE BY:
VELVET SPONGE CAKE

2 c. sugar
2½ c. flour
1 c. boiling water
2 tsp. baking powder
1 tsp. lemon
6 eggs, reserving 3 whites for icing

Beat the yolks a little, add the sugar and beat 15 minutes; add the 3 beaten whites, and the boiling water just before the flour; flavor, and bake in three layers, putting the icing between them.

Icing for Velvet Sponge Cake

3 egg whites
6 dessert spoons powdered sugar
flavor with lemon
Mix together.

MARCH 19

Don't bite the hand
that has your allowance in it.

*Your conscience does not necessarily prevent you
from doing wrong, but it does prevent you
from enjoying it.*

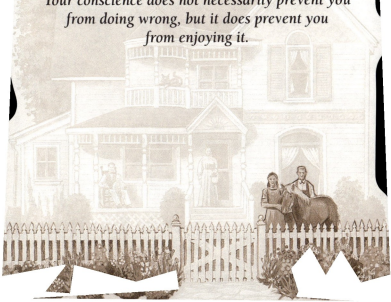

OCTOBER 14

Patience strengthens the spirit,
sweetens the temper, stifles anger,
and subdues the tongue.

What good is gossip if you can't repeat it?

MARCH 20

The best way we know to win an argument
is to start by being in the right.

*Sign at a day-care center:
Infants subject to change without notice.*

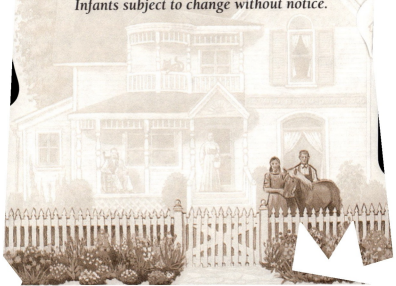

OCTOBER 13

Those who constantly look back
may know where they've been,
but not where they're going.

*A little inaccuracy sometimes saves
tons of explanation.*

MARCH 21

Home is where people grumble the most but are often treated the best.

A house divided makes many apartments.

OCTOBER 12

Many a man who pays rent all his life
owns his own home;
and many a family has successfully
saved for a home
only to find itself at last
with nothing but a house.

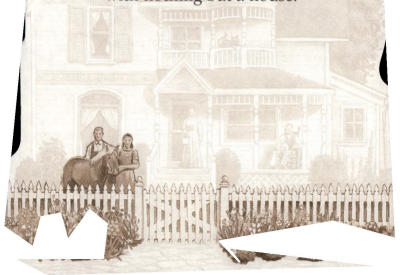

MARCH 22

Parenthood: That state of being better chaperoned than you were before marriage.

Most people meet their expenses easily — they are everywhere they go.

OCTOBER 11

Some parents are more pleased
to have children look like them
than act like them.

Cloning is the sincerest form of flattery.

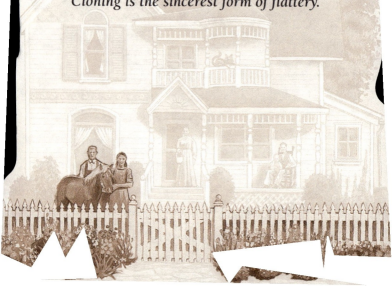

MARCH 23

People are lonely because they build walls instead of bridges.

Let today's opportunities shadow yesterday's disappointments.

OCTOBER 10

A child's lament:
If I'm noisy they spank me —
and if I'm quiet
they take my temperature.

*A "miracle drug" is any medicine
you can get the kids to take
without screaming.*

MARCH 24

Children have never been very good at listening to their elders, but they have never failed to imitate them.

— James Baldwin

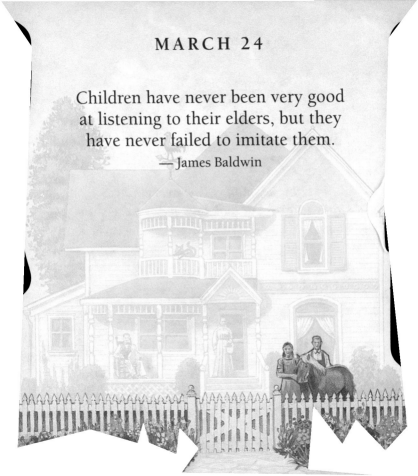

OCTOBER 9

Many homes have all the
newest labor saving devices,
but very few money saving devices.

*They say money isn't everything.
That's true — but look how many things it is.*

MARCH 25

Today is the tomorrow you worried about yesterday. Now you know why.

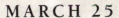

If God wanted us to have daylight savings time, He would have made it easier to reset the clocks.

OCTOBER 8

If you are not a charming conversationalist
you may still be a big hit
as a charmed listener.

*There are those who really should stop
shooting from the lip.*

MARCH 26

It is often a long way home,
but it is better than a short cut
to a mere lodging house.

*We understand so much about life
by looking back, but we must try
to look forward.*

OCTOBER 7

A good neighbor is a fellow
who smiles at you over the back fence
but doesn't climb over it.

MARCH 27

Some wives want their husbands
to know that a woman's work
is never done.
Some husbands ask why women
don't just start earlier.

OCTOBER 6

Love is a ticklish feeling
around the heart
that can't be scratched.

To understand a parent's love: have a child.
— Japanese proverb

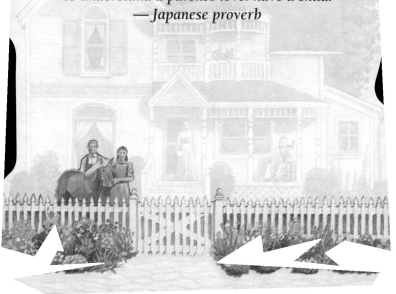

MARCH 28

Don't worry if grandparents
live in the past— it's a lot cheaper!

*Try to walk arm in arm with your loved ones,
even if you don't see eye to eye.*

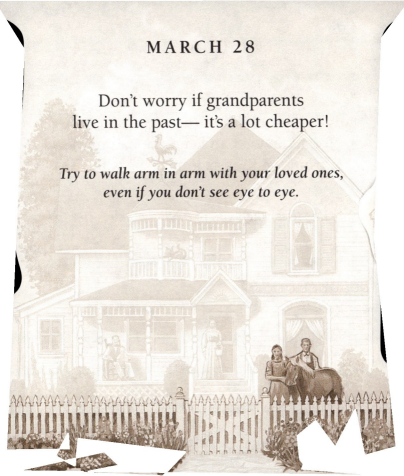

OCTOBER 5

It used to be that parents
taught their children the value of a dollar.
Today they try to keep the bad news
from the kids as long as possible.

Time flies when you're paying a babysitter.

MARCH 29

Middle age is when you are too young
to take up golf and too old
to rush up to the net.

*Lots of work around the house
is done in passing —
passing it on to someone else.*

OCTOBER 4

When you hear some of those rock groups,
you want to clap —
both your hands over your ears.

*These days it's better to face the music
than to have to listen to it.*

MARCH 30

A sweater is a garment worn by a child when the mother feels cold.

You cannot hurt your eyesight by looking on the bright side.

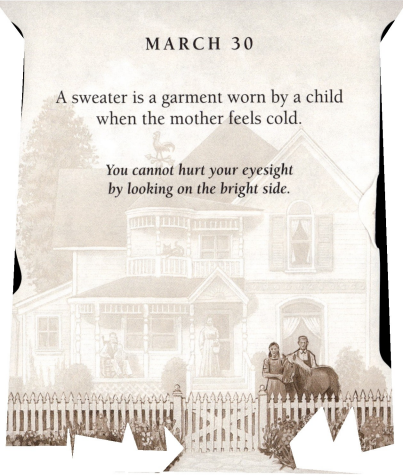

OCTOBER 3

The family is the one safe island
in an unknown sea.

*All things may come to those who wait,
but when they do, they're out of date.*

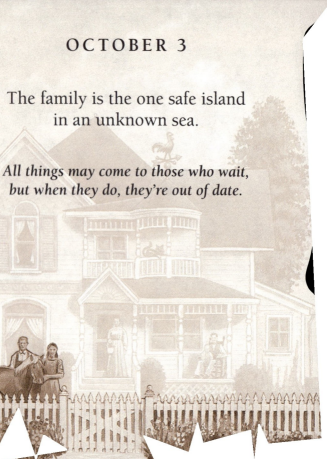

MARCH 31

Patience is what you get
after your children are grown.

*Some people sit down at mealtime
to continue eating.*

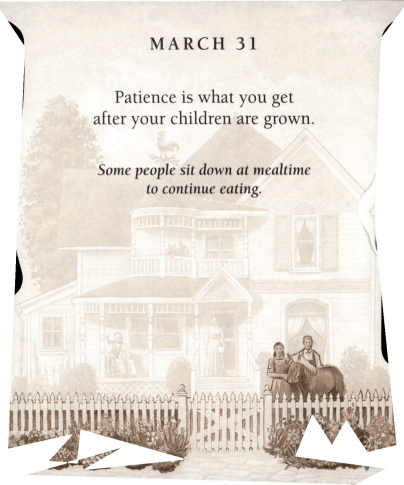

OCTOBER 2

Don't expect to enjoy life
if you keep the cream of human kindness
all bottled up.

*Nostalgia is the sandpaper that removes
the rough edges from the good old days.*

APRIL 1

Cleaning in the cold raw days of early spring disturbs everybody's comfort, and may endanger health, while cleaning late, after the spring days come, gives the moths an advantage, and adds much to the housekeeper's work and weariness.

— The Housekeeper Cookbook, 1884

OCTOBER 1

Good breeding is never more apparent
than at the table, and if the example
of the parents is correct, the training
of children in good manners
will be comparatively easy.

— The Housekeeper Cookbook, 1884

APRIL 2

God save us from bad neighbors
and from a beginner on the trombone.

*Today's family is a group of people,
no two of whom want to rent the same movie.*

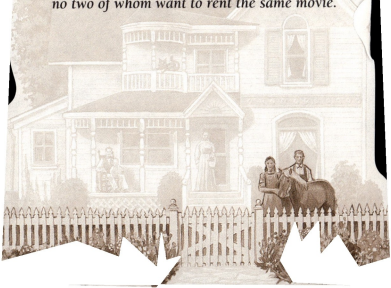

SEPTEMBER 30

Everyone thinks of changing the world,
but no one thinks of changing herself.

*Most people like the old days best —
they were younger then.*

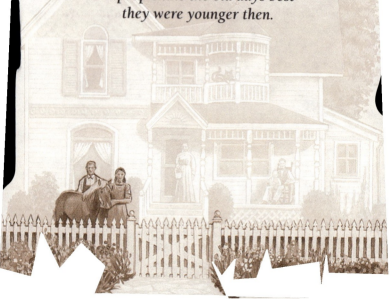

APRIL 3

Cast your bread upon the waters
and you'll get back ten soggy loaves.

*Daylight savings time is really an attempt
to keep us awake so we can spend more.*

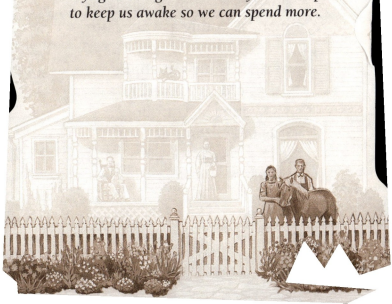

SEPTEMBER 29

Youth is not entirely a time of life;
it is a state of mind.
Nobody grows old by merely living
a number of years. People grow old
by deserting their ideals.
You are as young as your faith,
as old as your doubt;
as young as your self-confidence,
as old as your fear;
as young as your hope,
as old as your despair.

— Douglas MacArthur

APRIL 4

Out of the mouths of babes come the remarks parents wish they had never made in the first place.

Why do so many do-it-yourself projects involve more people than yourself?

SEPTEMBER 28

Enjoy today. Don't waste it grieving over a bad yesterday — tomorrow may be difficult.

Children will be children, even when they're fifty years old.

APRIL 5

The family is a tree which its members must remember to water.

A kind word spoken often travels on until it comes back to you.

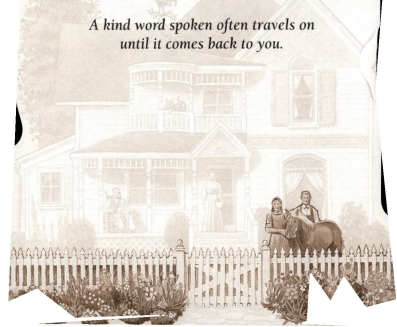

SEPTEMBER 27

It's good to have money
and all the things money can buy,
but it's good to check up once in a while
and make sure you haven't lost
the things that money can't buy.

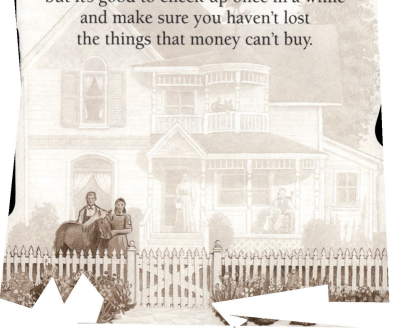

APRIL 6

A man travels the world over
in search of what he needs
and returns home to find it.

*Life often feels like moving day —
a temporary mess.*

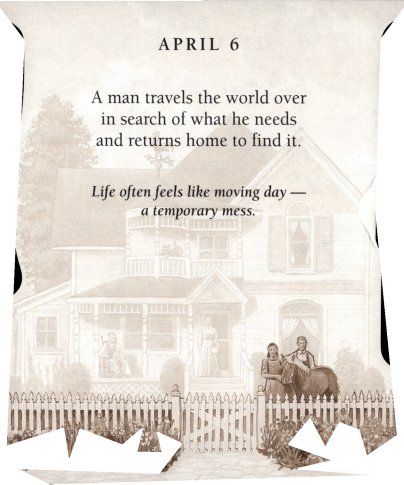

SEPTEMBER 26

Children are like wet cement —
whatever falls on them
makes an impression.

*One laugh of a child will bring a ray of light
to a dark day.*

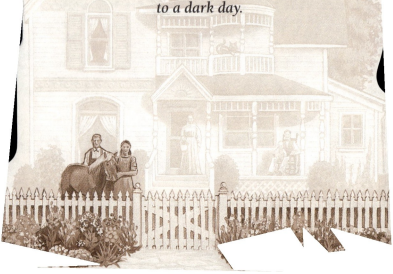

APRIL 7

One thing about church —
you're never too bad to come in
and you're never too good to stay out.

*Stand up to make a speech
and watch your mind
become inactive on the spot.*

SEPTEMBER 25

Don't worry about forgetting things
as you grow older
because you'll soon forget
what you forgot.

*Youth looks ahead, old age looks back,
and middle age looks tired.*

APRIL 8

The pride of ancestry increases
in the ratio of distance.

*A father is not someone to lean on
but someone who makes leaning unnecessary.*

SEPTEMBER 24

It might not be opportunity knocking —
it could be one of your relatives!

*A task worth doing and friends worth having
make life worthwhile.*

APRIL 9

People who live in stone houses
should never throw glasses.

*No matter what happened in the past,
the future is spotless.*

SEPTEMBER 23

The trouble with owning a home
is that no matter where you sit,
you're looking at something
you should be doing.

*You can't make a place for yourself under the sun
if you keep sitting in the shade of the family tree.*

APRIL 10

Most people are totally honest
— as long as you don't ask them
how their children are doing.

*Some families have got it all together
but they forgot where they put it.*

SEPTEMBER 22

Keeping peace in the family
requires patience, love, understanding
and at least two television sets.

*The only people you should want to get even with
are those who have helped you.*

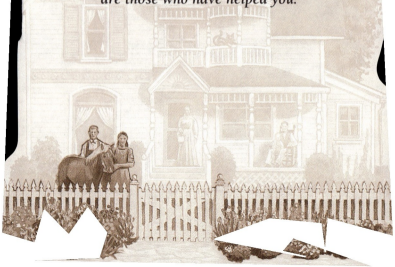

APRIL 11

There's this woman who is so neat
she puts paper under the cuckoo clock.

*The problem with living from the
school of experience is that
you never graduate.*

SEPTEMBER 21

If home is where the heart is,
some have some serious
circulatory problems.

Kindness is the signature of a loving heart.

APRIL 12

Dreams are free,
unless you want them to happen.

*The best angle to approach any problem
is the try-angle.*

SEPTEMBER 20

A good test of memory is to recall all the kind things you have said about your neighbor.

A small town is a place where every other person you meet is some kind of cousin.

APRIL 13

Thank goodness there's no good or bad in outer space — and there won't be until we put it there.

SEPTEMBER 19

After reading the epitaphs in the cemetery, you wonder where they bury the sinners.

What the world needs is an amplifier for the still, small voice.

APRIL 14

RECIPES FROM DAYS GONE BY:
ONION SALAD

Slice young onions and radishes; sprinkle a handful of salt over them and let them wilt half an hour. Wash off the salt, and squeeze out the water. Beat smooth some good sour cream, add sufficient vinegar to make it as sour as wished, pour it over the salad and sprinkle with pepper.

SEPTEMBER 18

I have everything now
I had twenty years ago —
except now it's all lower.
— Gypsy Rose Lee

*We never truly know the love of our parents
until we become parents ourselves.*

APRIL 15

Income tax returns:
the most imaginative fiction
written today.

*The IRS takes everything
but your imagination—
that will probably come next year.*

SEPTEMBER 17

The person who says
his troubles are all behind him
is probably a school bus driver.

*There is one thing we can do
all by ourselves — get lost.*

APRIL 16

Spring Cleaning

You wash all the windows
and scrub all the floors.
You polish up the handles
on the front and back doors,
You've aches in your fingers
and pains in your toes,
The place is tidied up now,
So next day it snows!

SEPTEMBER 16

While we've youth in our hearts,
we can never grow old.

*Age is a very high price to pay
for maturity.*

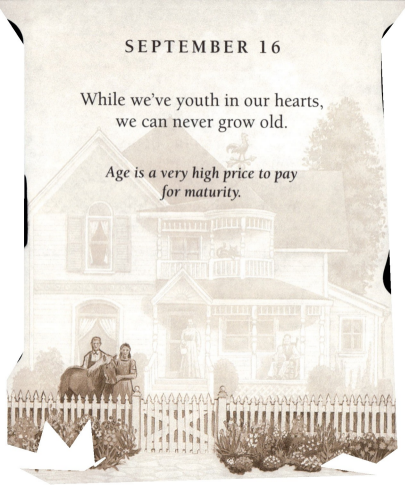

APRIL 17

The only difference between a rut and a grave is their dimensions.

Food for the mind should be chosen as carefully as food for the body.

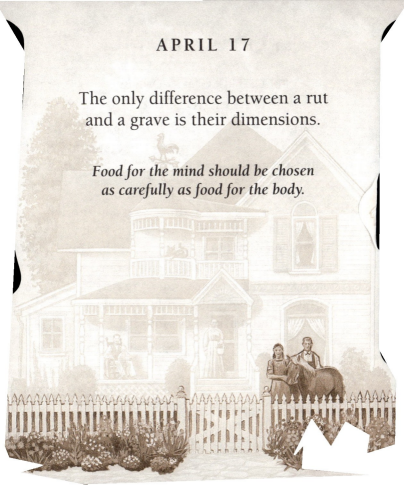

SEPTEMBER 15

RECIPE FROM DAYS GONE BY:
BUTTERED TAFFY

1 quart water   4 lbs. white sugar
1 lb. butter   1 tsp. cream of tartar
1 tablespoon vanilla extract

Boil sugar, water, and cream of tartar together, stirring all the time; then add vanilla or other flavoring. Boil to the crack, adding the butter, either cut in pieces or melted, and as soon as it is thoroughly incorporated and boiled into sugar, pour upon a greased marble slab; when sufficiently cool, turn in the edges and mark, or cut into squares.

APRIL 18

You may not remember this far back,
but once upon a time movies were rated
on how good they were,
not on who was allowed to see them.

SEPTEMBER 14

The person who invented the eraser
had the human race pretty well sized up.

To err is human — to admit it isn't.

APRIL 19

If life did not have its little battles,
there would be no victories.

In order to make a dream come true,
we have to wake up.

SEPTEMBER 13

The best way to get some kids' attention is to stand in front of the TV.

The trouble with sitcoms is that they induce sit-comas.

APRIL 20

You can learn many things from children:
like how much patience you have,
for instance.

Home is a family's filling station.

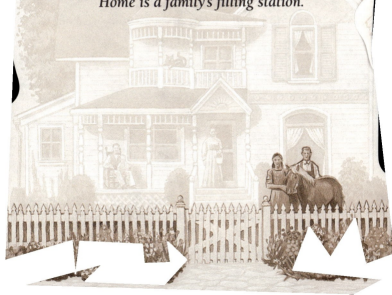

SEPTEMBER 12

The time to start worrying about children
is when they leave the house
without slamming the door.

*One rabbit to another:
"I don't care what people say —
I can't multiply."*

APRIL 21

The longer the grocery list,
the more likely it will be left at home.

*You can't always have everything,
but you can make the best of what you have.*

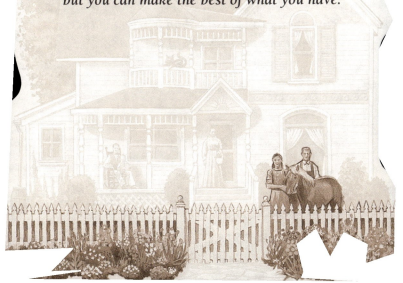

SEPTEMBER 11

The reason grandparents and grandchildren get along so well is that they have a common enemy.

— Sam Levenson

No superhero is faster than a grandmother pulling pictures out of her purse.

APRIL 22

Most don't want to be a millionaire,
we just want to live like one.

To stay youthful — stay useful.

SEPTEMBER 10

We've made great medical progress in the last century. What used to be merely an itch is now an allergy.

You grow up the day you have your first laugh — at yourself.

APRIL 23

The biggest room in some homes
is the room for improvement.

*Your home is a castle; just get an estimate
on replacing the siding and you'll agree.*

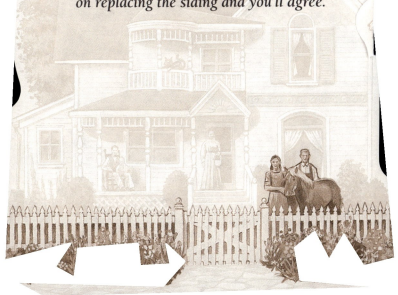

SEPTEMBER 9

The nicest things about new friends
is that they haven't heard our old stories.

*A smile is a powerful weapon —
you can even break ice with it.*

APRIL 24

Most of us are not confused,
just well mixed.

*The best way to let fish know
you want to catch them
is to drop them a line.*

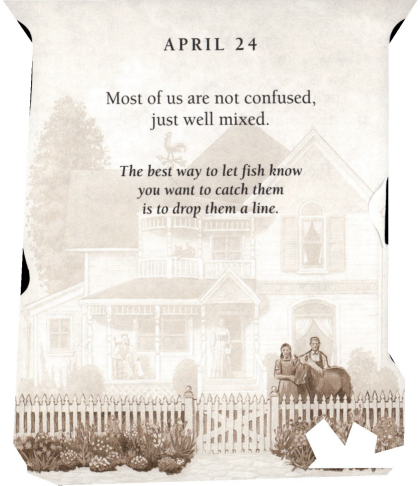

SEPTEMBER 8

There's nothing wrong with teenagers that reasoning with them won't aggravate.

The courage to speak must be matched by the wisdom to listen.

APRIL 25

Some people talk so much
they come back from a day at the beach
with a sunburned tongue.

*If your best friend is the family dog,
you're probably in the dog house.*

SEPTEMBER 7

If you don't attend other people's funerals,
you certainly can't expect them
to come to yours.

*Some people may grow old gracefully
but seldom gratefully.*

APRIL 26

Long walks are therapeutic, especially when taken by people who annoy us.

Remember when "naughty books" had to be read in the hay barn?

SEPTEMBER 6

September is when millions of bright,
shining, happy, laughing faces
turn toward school.
They belong to mothers and fathers.

APRIL 27

Even when you don't know
what you're doing,
do it well.

*It is much easier to be critical
than to be correct.*

SEPTEMBER 5

What our country really needs
is a child labor law designed
to keep them from working
parents to death.

A life of ease is a difficult pursuit.

APRIL 28

One of the mysteries of life is that
occasionally some piece of it
will be perfectly understandable.

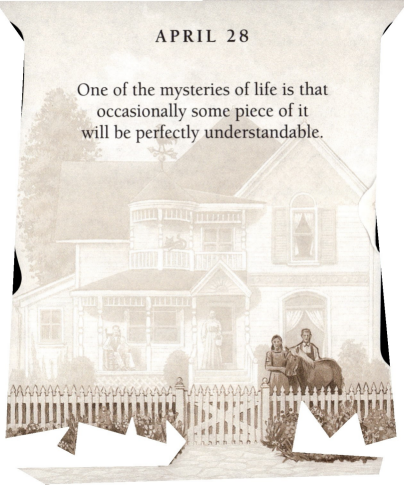

SEPTEMBER 4

Some people have the knack of saying what they think and getting out of the way before it's understood.

*Our grandparents had farms,
our parents had a garden,
but this generation has a can opener.*

APRIL 29

When you move from temptation's way, don't leave a forwarding address.

A clean basement usually means a cluttered garage.

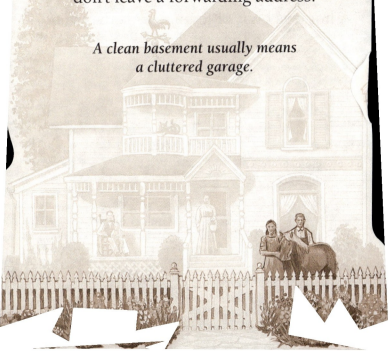

SEPTEMBER 3

A house is built of logs and stones,
of tiles and posts and tiers;
A home is built of loving deeds that stand
a thousand years.

APRIL 30

Climbing the ladder to success
is impossible with your hands
in your pockets.

In times of stress, rest, don't quit.

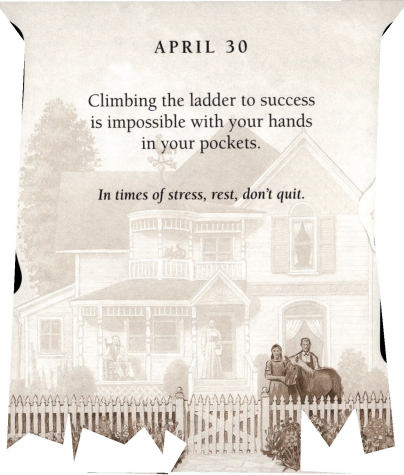

SEPTEMBER 2

Fifty years ago people thought television was impossible. Today many of us still do.

In some homes, the TV set is better adjusted than the kids.

MAY 1

Buy from respectable dealers
in the neighborhood, rather than
from transient and irresponsible parties,
for the dealer will rectify a mistake
at once; the other cannot be trusted.
— The Housekeeper Cookbook, 1884

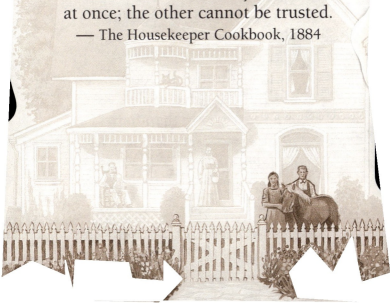

SEPTEMBER 1

The inner husks of corn
make a good underbed.
Oat straw is excellent.
Hair mattresses are best,
and in the end most economical.
Those made of coarse wool
are objectionable at first
on account of the odor
but are serviceable
and less costly than hair.
—The Housekeeper Cookbook, 1884

MAY 2

There's only one thing worse
than a flooded basement —
and that's a flooded attic.

A house is made with walls and beam;
a home is built with love and dreams.

AUGUST 31

Old age is like a plane
flying through a storm.
Once you're aboard,
there's nothing you can do.

— Golda Meir

MAY 3

Money may not bring happiness,
but wouldn't it be nice
to find out for yourself.

Nothing lasts forever — not even your troubles.

AUGUST 30

When you are young,
you dream of leaving your house
on a set of wheels.
When you retire you dream of living
in a house on a set of wheels.

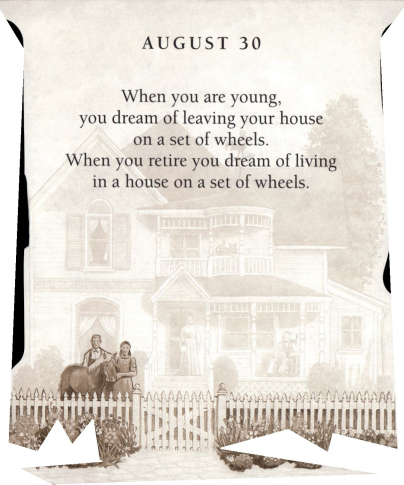

MAY 4

Motivation is when your dreams put on work clothes.

The only thing about kids having pets, is that the pets have children.

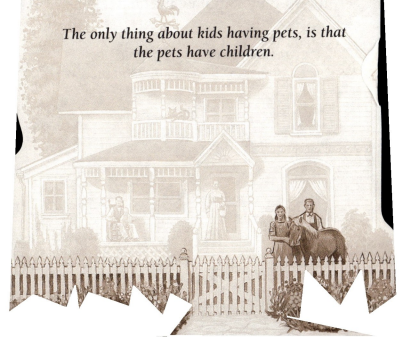

AUGUST 29

It doesn't really matter
who wears the pants in the family
just so there's money in the pocket.

*If food prices keep going up
soon TV dinners will cost more than the TV.*

MAY 5

An affluent neighborhood is one where Girl Scouts go door to door selling croissants. In the spring kids sign up for Little League polo. The Salvation Army band has a string section, and the bird feeders have a salad bar.

AUGUST 28

Almost all faults are more forgivable than the methods we use to hide them.

Hating people is like burning down your house to get rid of a rat.

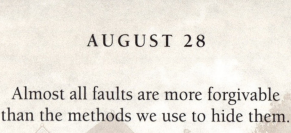

MAY 6

It takes a hundred soldiers
to make an encampment,
but one woman can make a home.

*In some families it would be best
if children were properly spaced —
about fifty feet apart.*

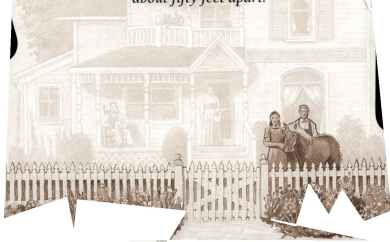

AUGUST 27

We should live in such a way
that we can laugh when we're together
and smile when we're alone.

*The art of memory
is the art of understanding.*

MAY 7

A mother's role is to deliver children — obstetrically once, and by car forever after.

What parents want is a breakfast cereal that takes the energy <u>out</u> of the child.

AUGUST 26

There are only two lasting lessons
we give our children —
one is roots and the other is wings.

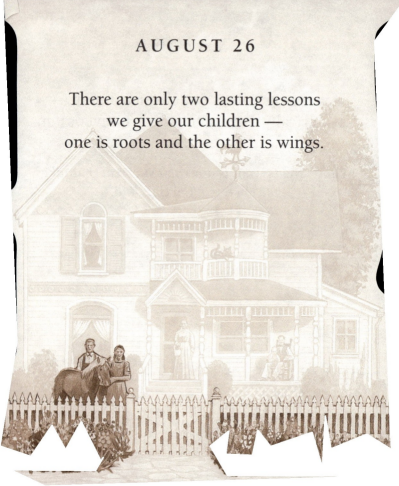

MAY 8

Did you hear the one about the salmon who's in a terrible state of depression? Every year she lays 10,000 eggs — come Mother's Day, not one card.

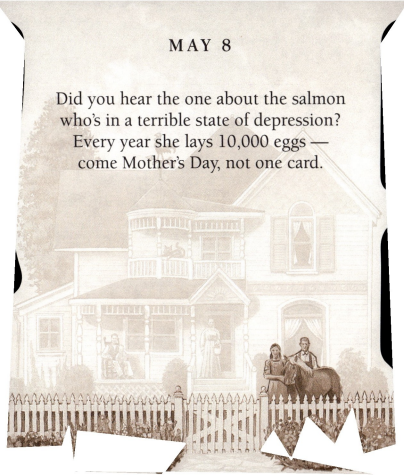

AUGUST 25

By the time you realize your parents were usually right, you have children who think you are usually wrong.

*Retirement is wonderful
if you have two essentials —
much to live on and much to live for.*

MAY 9

The head of the household is the one in possession of the remote control.

These days, a child answers back before a parent has said anything.

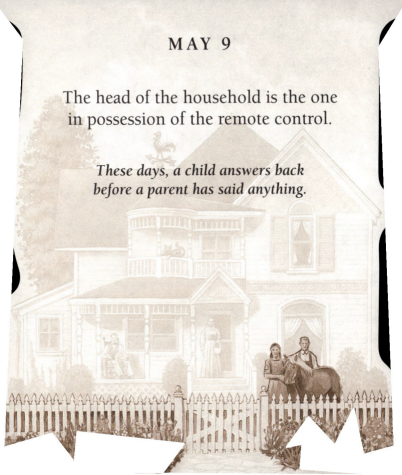

AUGUST 24

Everything in today's homes
is controlled by remote control —
except the children.

*Learn to speak kind words —
nobody resents them.*

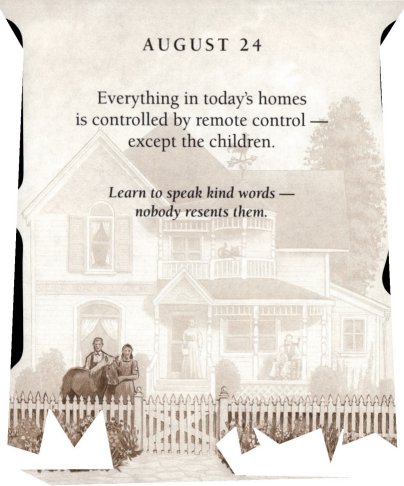

MAY 10

Allow children to be happy
in their own way, for what better way
will they ever find?

*Every day give yourself another chance
whether you deserve it or not.*

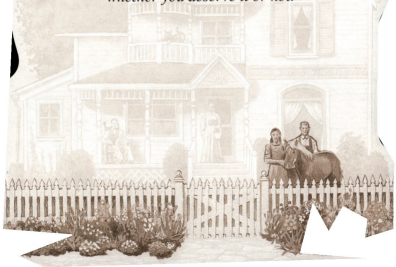

AUGUST 23

Forgiveness is the key that
unlocks the door of resentment
and the handcuffs of hate.
It is the power that
breaks the chains of bitterness
and the shackles of selfishness.

*The weaker the argument,
the stronger the words.*

MAY 11

It's impossible to keep a straight face while watching one or more puppies.

Conscience is what makes a boy tell his mother before his sister does.

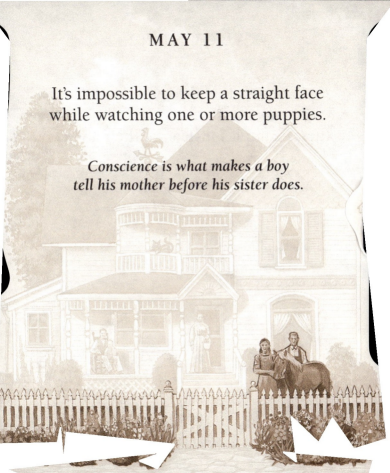

AUGUST 22

Parents should remember that
one day children will follow
their examples instead of their advice.

*A pint of examples
is worth a gallon of advice.*

MAY 12

Something else to remember
when you're doing house cleaning:
An ounce of spider's web
would extend 350 miles
if straightened out.

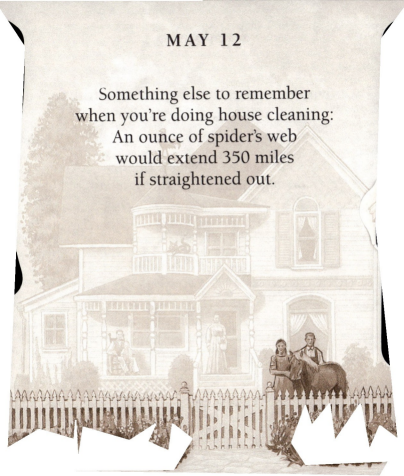

AUGUST 21

Love is the glue that cements a family;
arguing keeps it from sticking.

*Nothing seems to make children
more affectionate than sticky hands.*

MAY 13

Some day science may be able to explain
why a child can't walk around
a mud puddle.

*When we are flat on our backs,
there is no way to look but up.*

AUGUST 20

One reason parents want their children
to play piano instead of violin
is that it's much harder to lose a piano.

*Ignorance is no excuse —
it's the real thing.*

MAY 14

When some people talk about
their family tree,
they trim a branch off
here and there.

Let there be spaces in your togetherness.

AUGUST 19

Happiness is like potato salad —
when shared with others it's a picnic.

A bird in the hand is bad table manners.

MAY 15

RECIPE FROM DAYS GONE BY:
FRIED CUCUMBERS

Take young fresh ones, cut across if large, lengthwise if small, dip in egg and flour or bread crumbs, let stand 15 minutes and fry in boiling lard. When done place on a paper in the mouth of the oven.

AUGUST 18

Sending a child to college
is like buying a new car every year
and never getting to drive it.

*Adolescence is when children
start bringing up parents.*

MAY 16

The most important thing a father
can do for his children
is to love their mother.

— Father T. Hessburgh

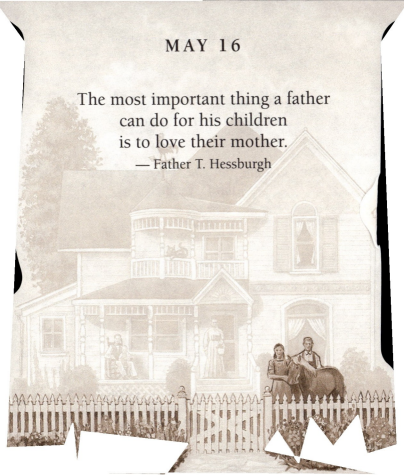

AUGUST 17

The world needs more warm hearts
and fewer hot heads.

Stay out of sight and you stay out of trouble.
— John F. Kennedy

MAY 17

There's the TV weatherman who was fired because he couldn't even predict yesterday's weather.

*Don't pray for rain
if you're going to complain about the mud.*

AUGUST 16

Reasoning with a child
is what gives you something to do
while discovering that you can't.

A fence between makes love more keen.

MAY 18

A family can bear up under a cataclysmic tragedy and go to pieces when the water has to be turned off for a few minutes.

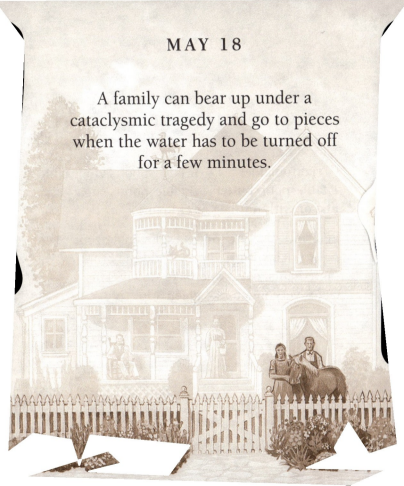

AUGUST 15

RECIPE FROM DAYS GONE BY:
TOMATO PIE

Green tomatoes   4 tablespoons vinegar
1 tablespoon butter   3 tablespoons sugar
Flavor with nutmeg or cinnamon

Peel and slice the tomatoes, lay in a deep plate lined with rich paste; add the other ingredients, cover and bake slowly. This tastes very much like green apple pie.

MAY 19

We must live so our memories
will be part of our happiness.

We have all forgotten more than we remember.

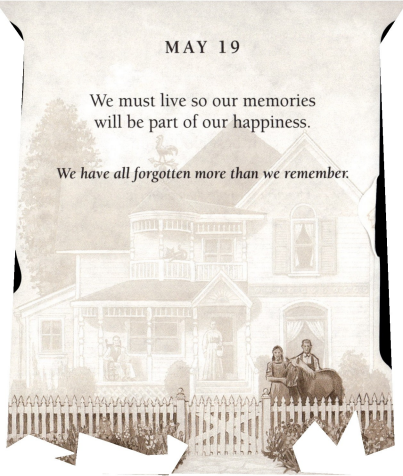

AUGUST 14

Out of the mouths of babes —
usually when you have
your best clothes on.

*The best thing to spend on children
is your time.*

MAY 20

There are two sides to every question we're not interested in.

A secret is something you tell to only one person at a time.

AUGUST 13

The only persons permitted to punish children should be persons who love them.
— Marlene Dietrich

MAY 21

If it hadn't been for Edison,
we'd be watching TV by candlelight.

Among the best home furnishings are children.

AUGUST 12

There's no use crying over spilled milk;
it only makes it salty for the cat.

*There's nothing thirstier
than a child who has just gone to bed.*

MAY 22

It's better to sleep on
what you intend to do
than stay awake all night
over what you did.

AUGUST 11

The ultimate economic and spiritual unit of any civilization is still the family.
— Clare Booth Luce

*To a young child,
there is no such period as between meals.*

MAY 23

If you feel like a fifth wheel,
remember the value of a spare tire
when someone has a flat.

*No man is as smart as he sounds
at his alumni dinner.*

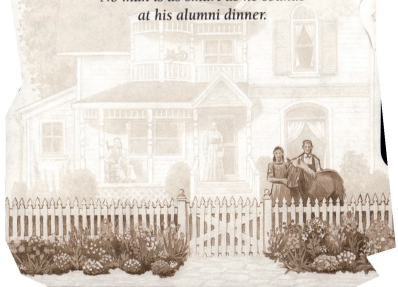

AUGUST 10

Some women are great housekeepers —
every time they get divorced,
they keep the house.

*One nice thing about going home
is that you don't have to make a reservation.*

MAY 24

Children are unpredictable —
you never know what inconsistency
they're going to catch you in next.

AUGUST 9

A mosquito is like a kid.
When he stops making noise,
he's on to something.

One thing children save up
for a rainy day is energy.

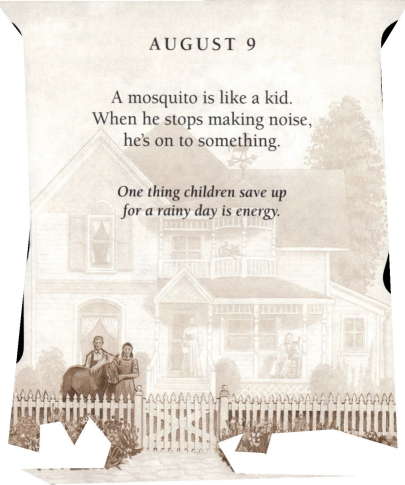

MAY 25

With the exception of world unrest nothing breaks out in more places than a garden hose.

If you're going to climb, you've got to grab the branches, not the blossoms.

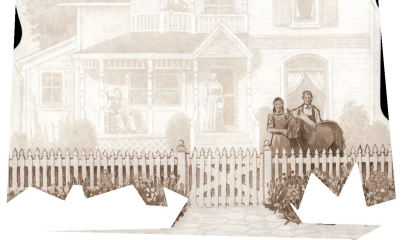

AUGUST 8

Just when you get the summer vacation paid off, it's time to think about Christmas presents.

Spills won't happen on a dirty floor.

MAY 26

Nowadays, people don't hire domestic help, they marry it.

A good way to forget your troubles is to help others out of theirs.

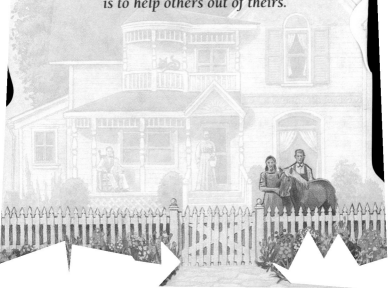

AUGUST 7

Middle age is when you still believe you'll feel better in the morning.

Some people's idea of housework is to sweep the floor with a glance.

MAY 27

The home is an extension of the owner, which explains why some homeowners get over-extended.

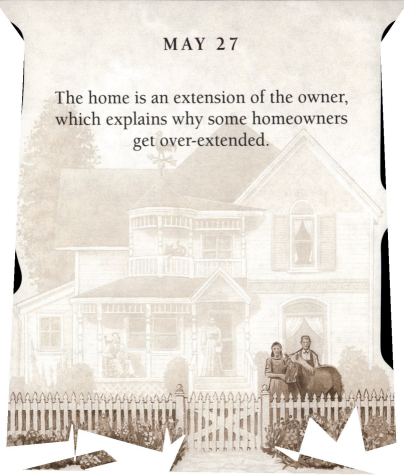

AUGUST 6

The only creatures who can sleep
standing up are horses
and parents of newborn babies.

*People who say they sleep like a baby
obviously never had one.*

MAY 28

These days, young people get too much of everything — including criticism.

*A child prodigy is one
with highly imaginative parents.*

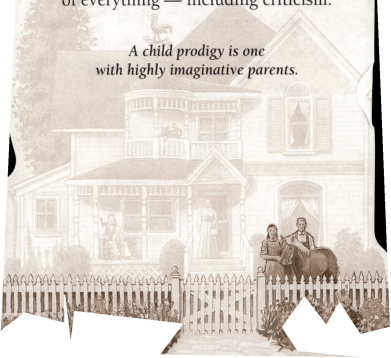

AUGUST 5

Home is the one place in all this world
where hearts are sure of each other.
It is the place of confidence.
It is the spot where expressions
of tenderness gush out
without any dread of ridicule.

— Fred W. Robertson

MAY 29

Many a man wishes he were strong enough to tear a telephone book in half — especially if he has teenage children.

The young know the rules,
but the old know the exceptions.

AUGUST 4

If you keep your head and heart
going in the right direction
you'll never have to worry about your feet.

*God should be a steering wheel,
not a spare tire.*

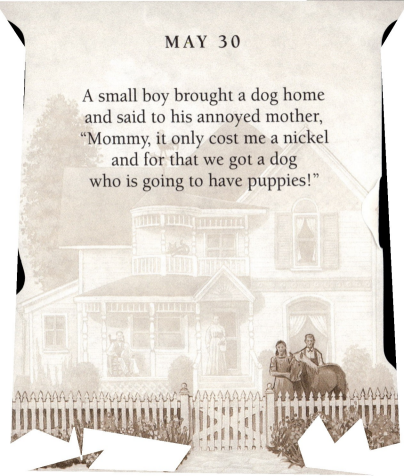

MAY 30

A small boy brought a dog home
and said to his annoyed mother,
"Mommy, it only cost me a nickel
and for that we got a dog
who is going to have puppies!"

AUGUST 3

Some people's idea of heaven
is nothing to do
and an eternity to do it in.

What's a halo?
It's just another thing
you have to keep polished.

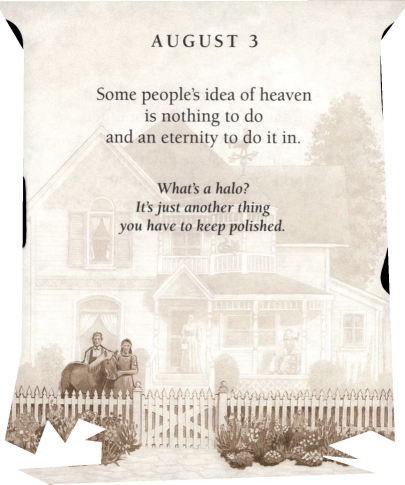

MAY 31

The best way to keep children at home
is to make the home atmosphere pleasant
and let the air out of the tires.

AUGUST 2

Fathers don't worry about their daughters
marrying some Tom, Dick, or Harry.
They worry she may marry some
Moe, Larry or Curley.

*Something every couple should save
for old age is marriage.*

JUNE 1

Two rules are considered binding
in good society: No gentleman should be
introduced to a lady unless her permission
has been previously given;
no woman should be introduced
formally to another woman
unless the introducer knows
it is mutually desired.

— The Housekeeper Cookbook, 1884

AUGUST 1

Table manners:
Do not lean on the table,
and avoid noisy behavior. Keep elbows close
to the side, and the feet in front of the chair.
Sit easily erect, with legs bent at the knee.

— The Housekeeper Cookbook, 1884

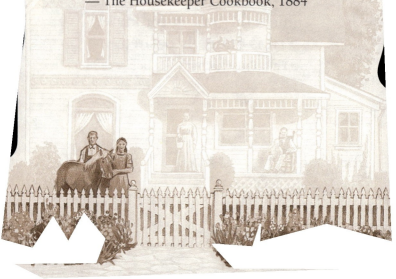

JUNE 2

When a mother explores a child's pockets, she generally gets what the average explorer does — enough evidence for a lecture.

Screen door:
Something the kids get a bang out of.

JULY 31

Reasoning with a child is fine
as long as you can reach the child's reason
without destroying your own.

*Let your children go
if you want to keep them.*

JUNE 3

A bride today has so many showers,
that all her friends get soaked —
some several times.

Works, not words, are the proof of love.

JULY 30

The recipe for happiness:
to have just enough money
to pay the monthly bills you acquire,
a little surplus to give you confidence,
a little too much work each day,
enthusiasm for your work,
a substantial share of good health,
a couple of real friends,
and a family to share
life's beauty with you.

— J. Kenneth Morle

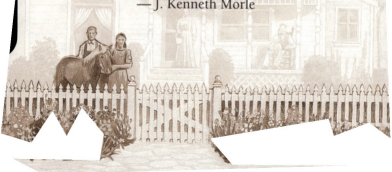

JUNE 4

If parents haven't learned anything from experience, they can always learn it from their children.

*Criticism is what you get
when you have everything else.*

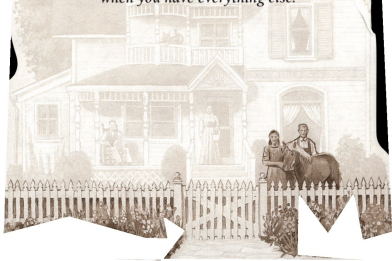

JULY 29

The best way to bring up children
is never to let them down.

*A house is not a home
when the owner is bound to roam.*

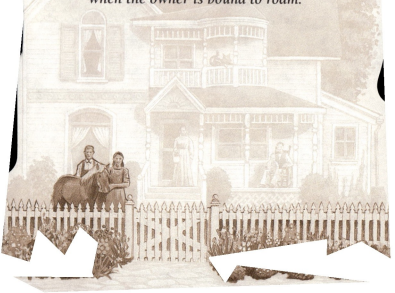

JUNE 5

There are three ways to get something done: do it yourself, hire someone to do it, or forbid a child to do it.

There are those who always hit the nail squarely on the thumb.

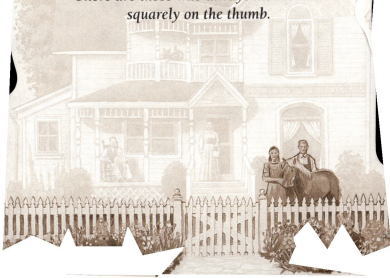

JULY 28

To keep young, stay around young people.
To get old, try to keep up with them.

*Children embarrass us in public
by behaving just like we do at home.*

JUNE 6

It is much classier to say we are moving in circles rather than running in circles, although it's really the same thing.

Stars can affect human lives.
They provide employment
to hundreds of astrologers.

JULY 27

Forgiveness saves the expense of anger,
the high cost of hatred,
and the waste of energy.

Saying it with flowers doesn't mean
throwing bouquets at yourself.

JUNE 7

Memory is a wonderful treasure
if you just know how to pack it.

*You are getting old
when you get winded playing checkers.*

JULY 26

Being young comes only once in life.
The trick is to make it last
as long as you can.

*People who have to ask for advice
probably don't have any close relations.*

JUNE 8

Etiquette means behaving yourself
a little better than is absolutely necessary.

*After a good meal
one can forgive anybody —
even one's relatives.*

JULY 25

Many people would rather
look backward than forward
because it is easier to remember
where they've been than to figure out
where they are going.

JUNE 9

Some give their kid ultimatums:
either mow the lawn or cut your hair.

*If a child lives with approval,
he learns to live with himself.*

JULY 24

These days it seems there are
more model homes than model families.

*It seems the only thing
that hasn't increased in cost
is free advice.*

JUNE 10

It's great for children to have pets until the pets start having children.

Man is a dog's ideal of what God should be.

JULY 23

Just as the gardener is responsible
for the products of her garden,
so the family is responsible
for the character of its children.

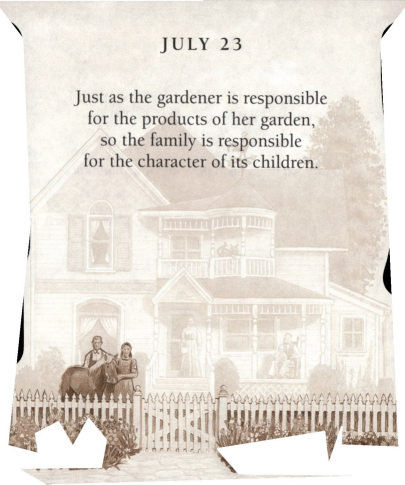

JUNE 11

More children are spoiled because the parents won't discipline grandma.

No man believes genius is hereditary until he has a child.

JULY 22

Many a family argument has been saved by the doorbell.

The kindest people are those who forgive and forget.

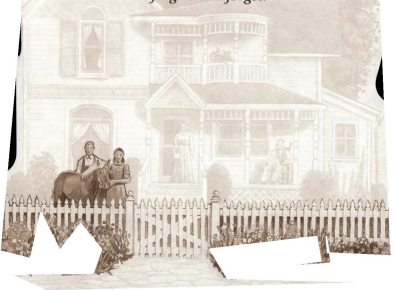

JUNE 12

Mixed emotions are what you have when your kids borrow ten dollars from you to buy you a Father's Day present.

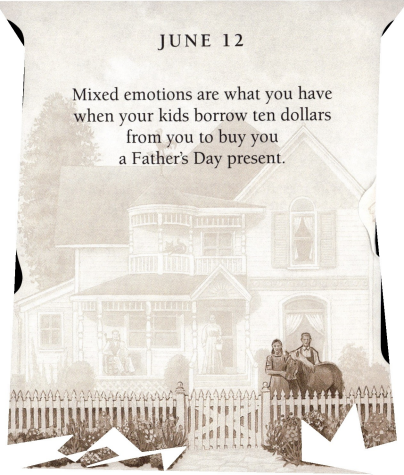

JULY 21

Happiness grows at our own firesides
and is not to be picked
in strangers' gardens.

With a small child, cleanliness is not next to godliness, it's next to impossible.

JUNE 13

Why is it kids ride bicycles, run, play ball, set up a camp, swing, climb on trees, swim and race for eight hours . . . yet have to be driven to the garbage can?

JULY 20

The only things that children wear out faster than shoes are parents.

Two is company. Three is the result.

JUNE 14

He is the happiest, be he king or peasant, who finds peace in his home.

— Goethe

Happy homes are built with blocks of patience.

JULY 19

Believe me, there's nothing to playing an accordion. Anyone who can fold a road map can play an accordion.

Laughter is the sweetest music that ever greeted the human ear.

JUNE 15

RECIPE FROM DAYS GONE BY:
IMPERIAL NECTAR

1 quart water
1¼ ounces tartic acid
1 teaspoon flour
1¼ pounds sugar
⅓ ounce gum arabic
5 egg whites

Dissolve acid, gum arabic, and sugar in the water; beat the whites of eggs and flour thoroughly; then add one-half cup of water. When the syrup is blood-warm, add the whites; boil 3 minutes. Take 2 tablespoons of syrup to two thirds of a glass of water; add one-third teaspoon bi-carbonate of soda; stir well.

JULY 18

No one grows old by living —
only by losing interest in living.

*You must arrange in advance
for pleasant memories.*

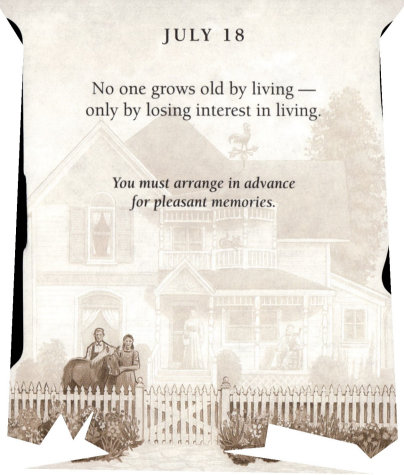

JUNE 16

Why pay money to have your family tree traced? Go into politics and have the media do it for you.

Kids, do something your mother will always be grateful for: move out.

JULY 17

Some of today's happiest reunions occur when the children find their parents at home.

Happiness in the home depends upon the ability to overlook.

JUNE 17

The best way to get rid of garbage
is to gift wrap it and leave it
near an open window
when you park your car at the mall.

JULY 16

No matter how thin you slice it,
it's still baloney.

*Nothing lasts as long as a box of cereal
that kids don't like.*

JUNE 18

When you're a kid, the scary sounds
come from under your bed.
When you're an adult, the scary sounds
come from under the hood of your car.

JULY 15

RECIPE FROM DAYS GONE BY:
LEMON JELLY

½ box gelatin
½ pint cold water
3 lemons, juice
1 pint boiling water
1½ cups sugar

Soak the gelatin in the cold water 1 hour, add the boiling water, sugar, and juice of lemons; let stand on the stove till boiling, strain into molds and set in a cool place until ready to serve. The addition of a few slices of lemon a few moments before straining improves the flavor.

JUNE 19

When family members make a mistake don't rub it in — rub it out.

Even God cannot make two mountains without a valley in between.

JULY 14

You may be a nobody to most people. What really matters is being somebody to everybody who's somebody to you.

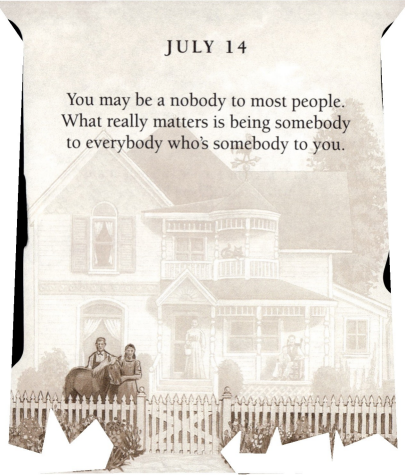

JUNE 20

Marriage is that relation between man and woman in which the interdependence is equal, the dependence is mutual, and the obligation reciprocal.

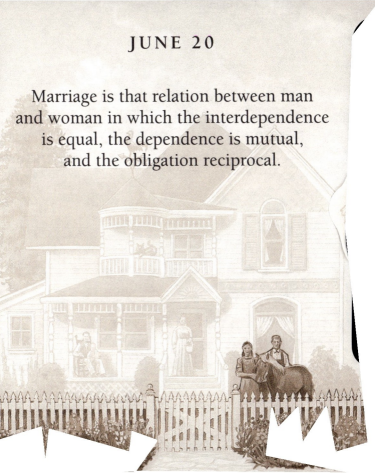

JULY 13

Show me an adult who can smile through a rock and roll concert, and I'll show you a hearing aid with weak batteries.

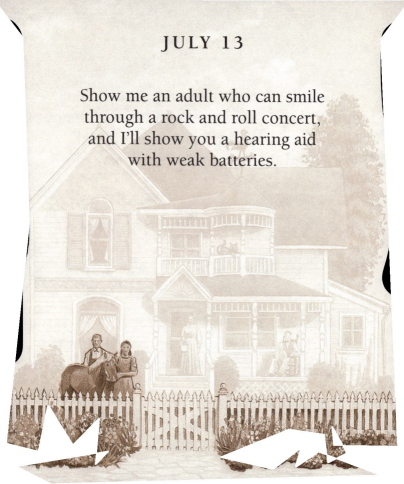

JUNE 21

The trouble with some
who say they can forgive and forget
is that they keep reminding others
they're doing it.

*Don't talk about yourself;
it will be done when you leave.*

JULY 12

A good memory test is to recall all the kind things you've said about your neighbor.

People who live in glass houses make interesting neighbors.

JUNE 22

There isn't anything that breaks up a family faster than people publishing their memoirs.

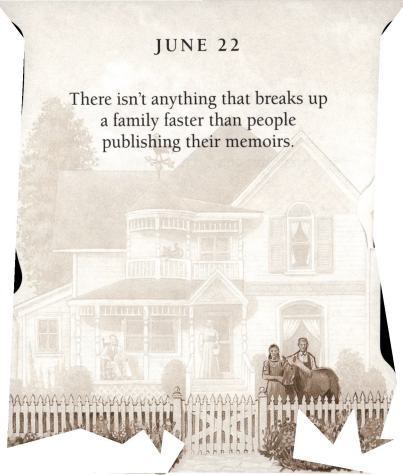

JULY 11

It's great to have all those new gadgets
in the house; but it's scary
having things around
that are smarter than you are.

Children are our most valuable resource.

JUNE 23

Sometimes your household budget
is right on target,
but sometimes it's a near myth.

*A necessity is almost any luxury
you see in the home of a neighbor.*

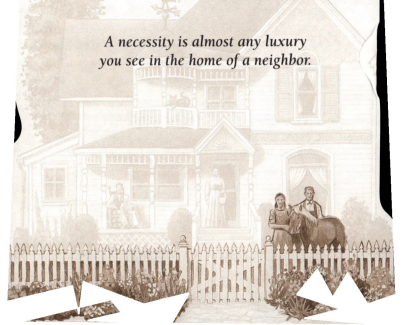

JULY 10

Middle age is when,
whenever you go on a holiday,
you pack a sweater.

Fairy Tale: Once upon a time there was a teenager who took the garage keys and came out with the lawn mower.

JUNE 24

If he takes you home
to meet his computer —
be prepared, he's ready to
pop the question.

*Computers can solve all kinds of problems
except the unemployment they create.*

JULY 9

Grandmas generally agree
that nobody is perfect,
but they're quick to point out
that the rule doesn't necessarily apply
to grandchildren.

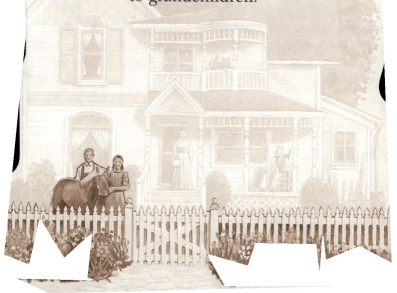

JUNE 25

We all have the same
major health problem —
it's something called being mortal.

JULY 8

People remain immature,
whatever their age,
as long as they think of themselves
as an exception to the human race.

JUNE 26

The trouble with owning a home is that no matter where you sit, you're looking at something you should be doing.

If a man had as many ideas during the day as he does when he has insomnia, he'd make a fortune.

JULY 7

A lot of today's frustration
is caused by a surplus of simple answers,
coupled with a tremendous
shortage of simple problems.

*People think something's worth believing
only if it's hard to believe.*

JUNE 27

You know your children are growing up when they stop asking for allowance and start asking for a loan.

Moving is the experience of pack up or pitch out.

JULY 6

To maintain a joyful family
requires much from both the parents
and the children. Each member
of the family has to become, in
a special way, the servant of the others.

— Pope John Paul II

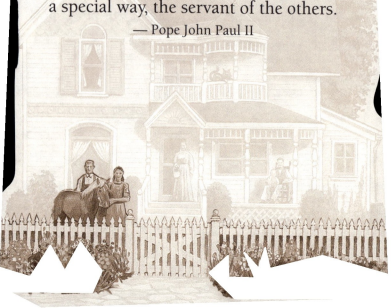

JUNE 28

When some are young they are so wild
they are impossible.
When they are old they act like a saint
and become impossible again.

JULY 5

Do not try to produce an ideal child;
it would find no fitness in this world.
— Herbert Spencer

*Why is it some people without children
always know just how you should raise yours?*

JUNE 29

The reason people remember
the "good old days"
is that there were so few of them.

*Genealogy is the science of tracing yourself
back to people better than you are.*

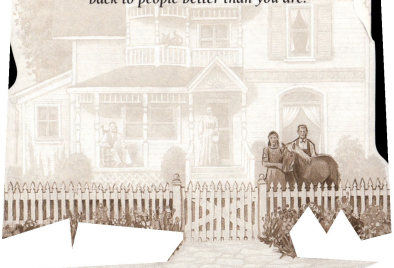

JULY 4

We must stop talking about
the American dream and start listening
to the dreams of Americans.

*Be the first to say
"Hello! Good to see you."*

JUNE 30

He may have a greasy hat
and his trousers may be shiny,
but if his children have their noses
flattened against the windowpane
a half-hour before he is due home
for supper, you can trust him
to be a good man.

JULY 3

I only know two tunes:
One is Yankee Doodle and the other isn't.
— U.S. Grant

Never forget that time spent with your children is never wasted.

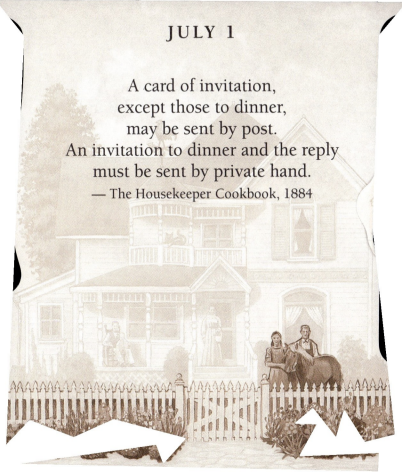

JULY 1

A card of invitation,
except those to dinner,
may be sent by post.
An invitation to dinner and the reply
must be sent by private hand.

— The Housekeeper Cookbook, 1884

JULY 2

If your home is overheated,
maybe you need prayer-conditioning.

*The middle years of marriage are the most critical.
In the early years, spouses want each other and
in the late years, they need each other.*

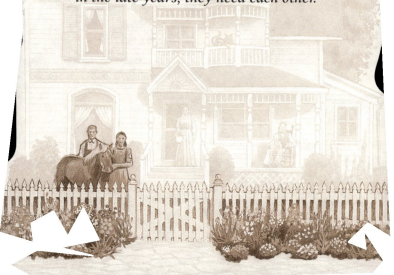